THE SECRET LIFE OF A
PREACHER'S WIFE

SHIRLEY

WestBow
P R E S S
A DIVISION OF THOMAS NELSON

WestBow Press books may be ordered through booksellers or by contacting:

WestBow Press
A Division of Thomas Nelson
1663 Liberty Drive
Bloomington, IN 47403
www.westbowpress.com
1-(866) 928-1240

ISBN: 978-1-4497-5355-9 (sc)
ISBN: 978-1-4497-5356-6 (e)

Library of Congress Control Number: 2012909244

Printed in the United States of America

WestBow Press rev. date: 11/02/2012

To the Memory of:
My Deceased Family

Dedicated to the Greatest
Joys of my Life
My Children

Presented To
Abused Women All Over the World
Incarcerated Women of Domestic Violence

In Memory of
All Ladies who lost Their Lives because of Domestic Violence

CONTENTS

Introduction   ix
Chapter 1   The Beginning   1
Chapter 2   The Engagement   17
Chapter 3   The Wedding   37
Chapter 4   After the Honeymoon   51
Chapter 5   Married Life Begins   55
Chapter 6   Going Home to Have the Baby   73
Chapter 7   A Short Vacation   83
Chapter 8   A Close Call   87
Chapter 9   Having Baby Number Three   91
Chapter 10   Having Baby Number Four   97
Chapter 11   Having Baby Number Five   103
Chapter 12   Starting a New Business   109
Chapter 13   Moving To Mississippi   119
Chapter 14   Living In a Condemned Trailer   123
Chapter 15   A Journey around the Country   131
Chapter 16   The Alleged Affair - The Depression   139
Chapter 17   Living Life on the Edge   149
Chapter 18   Becoming a New Me!   151
Chapter 19   The Conclusion   163

INTRODUCTION

I AM SHIRLEY AND I am a victim of domestic violence. That is to say, I was physically, mentally, and spiritually abused by my husband. I was married on April 1982 and walked out of an abusive marriage on September 9, 2006.

Although the physical abuse stopped in 2003 the mental and spiritual abuse continued.

In this book you will read about instances of abuse that took place in my marriage. It will be impossible and unnecessary to recount every time I was hit or mentally abused. The times are numerous.

My story is about the secrets I kept from the world, the shame, the hurt and the pain I hid deep within myself.

My story is about the secret life of a preacher's wife, me! For twenty-one years I prayed and asked God, "why?" Why was he allowing me to go through such agony? I knew Satan was causing this, but yet God allowed it. I knew any given day God could have put a stop to this. I also realize that whatever a Christian goes through it is so one day Gods' name will be glorified.

One night in the midst of my sleep, God woke me up and spoke to me in a vision.

He answered the question why I have suffered the years of abuse. He told me to write this book, he told me to write about the abuse and let preachers' wives and other ladies know that he did not want them to go through such suffering and pain. He said when you write this book, I want you to use this title:

"The Secret Life of A Preachers' Wife"

For almost a year I pleaded with my husband to support me in writing this book. It was my belief if we both could be open and honest about the things we did wrong in our marriage then God would heal our marriage. He would use us all over the world to help other people, married or unmarried. He denies all of his actions and chooses at this time to live in denial. This book is not an attempt to seek vengeance against my husband, it is not to embarrass, disgrace, humiliate, tear down, destroy or hurt him in any way.

Actually, this book is derived from our personal story, but it is no longer about us. It's to deliver, correct, regenerate, and save others from a life of abuse.

I have deliberately and intentionally not talked about my children a lot in this book. I am reserving their rights to tell their story in their own way and their own time.

I have a love for him, although we are no longer together. A part of me will always love the father of my wonderful five children.

I too have forgiven him for any and all wrong he did toward me.

It is my hope that the mistakes in our marriage will help you walk in the other direction. Know that it is not Gods' will for any of you to be abused.

CHAPTER 1

THE BEGINNING

I AM NUMBER SIX OF seven siblings. We grew up in a small rural area. Unlike, most people around us we never suffered for anything-food, clothes, or shelter. We had a stay at home mom, and one of the hardest working fathers you will ever know. He worked for the county, raised a farm where he sold everything from watermelons to hot peppers. He also would come home most evenings and cut pulpwood to sale.

He taught us all a valuable lesson; you can have what you need if you are willing to work for it.

For the most part my sisters and brothers were very outgoing, however I was timid, shy, and had a low self-esteem from a very young age. I guess I was an okay looking kid, I had peachy skin with rosy cheeks, thick long black curly hair, that gave me fits when my mom would comb it, and believe it or not I was very skinny.

Here's where my life began as I know it. At age five the Monday after the fourth Sunday in August I began my first day of school. About 6:45 a.m. the big yellow bus 69 drove up and stopped in our drive way. The very second I saw it I started to scream, cry, and have the worst temper tantrum possible. I was scared, afraid I had never been away from my mom. I didn't need to go to school, my mom had taught me to count, my alphabets and I could even write my name S H I R L E Y. So, what else I needed to know.

Well, with the help of my brothers and other young men on the bus they managed to get me on a seat and close the door. I cried and had a fit every school morning for at least a couple of months. I would cry so bad in class that my teacher would have to send for my oldest sister. She would take me to class with her where her friends spoiled me rotten.

One morning she took me to my classroom already bellowing my head off, my teacher was waiting for me, she told my oldest sister, who was sixth grade to go on to class. She said, "Young lady! I am going to break you this morning! Sit in the red chair, the hot chair." I sat down and she took a fan belt off a car and whipped me good. The next morning when the bus drove up I started crying again. My mom surprised me, she came outside, I was so happy thinking she was coming for me. She was coming for me alright she took a switch from behind her back and whipped me real good! Thanks to my mom and my teacher I didn't cry any more. Each year all the way through twelfth grade I would cry on the first day I just wouldn't let anyone see me. I went through all my years of school never having a boyfriend, a first kiss, and was not allowed to go to prom or anything. My dad was as strict as HELL.

Sometimes now I'm told I didn't have a boyfriend because I was so ugly. I had many opportunities with some very cute boys but I respected my dad's rules and although my dad never hit me once I didn't want to give him a reason to.

After graduating from high school, I worked on a summer job at a day care center until it was time to enroll in college. My baby brother took me to the school in his cool white '65 Ford Mustang.

We were there all day long. When I went to purchase my books something happened, all those years of being scared in school came back on me, I chickened out, I burst into tears and begged my brother to take me home. He said, "Mama and Daddy are going to kill you but come on." I guess Mama should have been there with her switch again.

I cried all the way home while he was trying his best to say everything he could to cheer me up.

My parents were much more understanding than we expected. My mom was so hurt and my dad but they said, it's your life but find you a job if you want to stay here. I found two jobs hated them both and quit both of them.

Three months later I gave my life to Christ and asked God to direct me from then on. I got a job as a cashier in a local store in a little city. I got to meet many people of all races. The pay was rotten but I loved this job with a passion. This job will play a "big role in my life as you will see if you read on."

One Sunday a lady named Jean came to visit our church service, I took an active role in my church, singing, praying, shouting, testifying you name it. My brother and I had been traveling everywhere since age 12 and he was 15 or 16, we were known all over the little country areas as the singing and praying kids.

Much against my dad's will, I started going to different churches with Jean every Sunday. We had a worship service once a month at our church so she would pick me up after Sunday school, and we'd go to two or three services every Sunday with her pastor. He preached at two or three churches every Sunday, he would always allow me to sing and help him pray for people.

I loved my life, I was happy my life was fulfilled. My brother and I formed bible classes, prayer meetings and even neighborhood prayers where a group of us along with Jean would go to the elderly homes and sing and pray once a week.

I guess Jean was about forty years older than me but she was my best friend, a second mom, an older sister, you get the point.

Well, that's the beginning of my life, now the secrets began.

I told you I would tell you how not going to college and going to work in the dollar store was a part of God's plan.

I was standing at the register one day when a strange young man came in whom I'd never seen before. He kept staring and I would pretend to look the other way. Finally he asked could he talk to me for a few minutes, so I asked my boss to take care of the customers for me, well, a few minutes turned into a few hours. He knew exactly who my family was If you ever see my sisters and brothers you'll see what I mean, our Mama and others would say daddy marked every one of us. We look alike, talk alike and probably think alike. Mom had seven beautiful curly head kids.

He asked about all my sisters and brothers, he finished school with my oldest sister, we talked about some of her old boyfriends (her and my baby sister wasn't as scared of Daddy as I was). He told me about his family, he was home visiting from Houston, Texas. I had gone to school with two of his younger sisters. He was preaching in a revival and wanted me to attend but I was unable to do so. Well, months passed by and Jean and I went to church one Sunday we arrived a few minutes late, someone was praying so we had to stand outside the door. I joked with her that he must have been white, because of the smoothness and the calmness in his voice, there was not any of the rhythm and hoop of the country black ministers in his voice. We both very ignorantly thought he was boring. When we were allowed in I immediately recognized him. It was the young minister that knew most of my family.

I had to sing before the sermon and afterward helped with the altar call as usual.

We spoke after church and talked a few minutes and he left. He was driving one of the most beautiful cars a country girl had ever seen. It was a mauve and burgundy Lincoln with a sunroof top. He was dressed as bad as his car but for some reason he was downright ugly to me. I grew up with masculine, brothers with huge afros, facial hair and downright cute. They were often called, The Jackson 5. It was hard to look at a man with kinky hair, no facial hair, and skinny as attractive. In other words I had no interest in him, and I'm sure he did not have any in me either.

Life was still good to me but I would soon be turning 22, I had no boyfriend yet. By now I have probably had two hundred men trying to be my first but it was out of the question. I was determined I would not kiss any one or be intimate with anyone unless we were married. At this time I had had several proposals, all of which I said a very quick no to.

My friend Jean thought one of the young men were perfect for me. He was tall, about my color, a Methodist preacher, and as handsome as Denzel Washington. However, even with all he had going for him, somehow I knew he wasn't for me. He had one of the best singing voices imaginable. Ideally we would have been perfect together in the flesh. He married another young lady, a few years later, became a pastor and a teacher.

Well, accepting the fact that he was not the one, I decided to start confronting God about a husband. On a cold Tuesday night in October, 1981, my brother, a few others and I came together for prayer at our home church. When it was my time to pray, I did something I had never done before, I literally talked to God face to face, I said to him "Lord, I'm lonely and I'm tired, send me a company keeper, someone to love me, Lord, please send me a husband and let him be a preacher, a real preacher not a jackleg, thank you Lord, Amen."

Well, that night the spirit spoke to me on the way home and told me he was sending me a husband, I walked in the house, tears was pouring down my face, the first thing my daddy said was, "She been at that church, shouting and acting a damn fool again. I told you her ass is stone crazy."

Daddy didn't understand a lot about the spirit of God until years later when he became born again himself.

Mama pleaded for him to leave me alone. I told her and my Aunt who had recently had cancer and was staying with us so we could take care of her.

I said, "Don't worry about anything, I'll be moving out soon, God spoke to me tonight and said he's sending me a husband, I'm going to be getting married."

Mama and Daddy left to go somewhere and my Aunt had a long heart to heart talk with me. She believed me and encouraged me to keep the faith and hold on to my belief. I went to bed so happy, with so many thoughts, guessing who it would be. I had no doubt God would keep his word.

The next morning I got up still excited and full of joy, got dressed and left for work. When I walked in my co-workers noticed the glow on my face and asked me what had me so happy. I just smiled and went about my daily task. At about 10:30 or 11:00 a.m. the phone rang. My boss said, "Shirley, telephone." My mom was the only person whom would ever call me at work so I said, "Tell her I'll call her right back."

My boss said, "It's not your mom, its long distance, it's a MAN!"

"Yeah right!" I said.

"I promise, Come on its long distance."

I nervously, hesitatingly went picked up the phone. "Hello, this is Shirley, how can I help you." A very pleasant, very soft spoken, very intelligent voice replied, "Hi Shirley, you probably don't remember me, I met you some months ago and we had a long conversation. I invited you to hear me preach in a revival. On last night I was praying for a wife and God put you on my heart. The spirit spoke to me and said call you."

By now, I'm shaking in my shoes, I asked him to hold on, I went talked to my boss and told her what he said, she said get back on the phone he could be real.

"I'm back," I said, my eyes were bucked my mouth was wide open; I could not believe what I was hearing. Then suddenly a thought came to me, it's a joke, this is your brother playing games with you because of your prayer last night. He has always been a prankster and through some of the roughest times we've been through-including sickness and death he has always managed to keep us laughing. I asked him how you can prove that you are the person you say you are. He described himself, he told me what we talked about, he described his car and he even mentioned the time we talked at the church.

He said if you will give me your number I will call you at home around seven p.m. I gave him the number and we said good-bye. I immediately called my mother and told her what happened. She said maybe God had answered my prayer. My reply was yeah right. Somehow I still thought my brother was playing a joke on me. Mama said it could not possibly be your brother because he was at work. I was pretty nervous the rest of the day anxiously waiting for my work day to be over. At 6:00 p.m. my daddy picked me up from work like every day. Unfortunately, Daddy and I did not have a relationship where I could tell him the big news. As a matter of fact he was so strict until I couldn't really take phone calls from boys, although I was twenty-one years old. My sister in law was waiting by the phone just like me. We had a very close friendship, you might say we were buddy, buddy. She was urging everything on, telling me to say this and say that and I was just sitting there laughing. We were both watching the clock and waiting for the phone to ring. About two minutes pass seven p.m. the phone rang, it was him. She answered the phone, "Shirley, It's for you."

I took the phone shaking like a leaf on a tree, we talked about fifteen minutes, and he said I work nights so I have to rest but I'll call you when I wake up. I personally think that she was more excited than me. I was still a doubter, still thinking it's absolutely no way God answered my prayer that quickly.

About 8:30pm or 9pm the phone rang, it was him, by this time I had talked to my brother and he came up with a brilliant idea. He told me to ask for his phone number and call him right back. He said if he's for real he'll answer the phone when you call him back. Well, I did just that, at first I dialed the wrong number and a Mexican man answered the phone. My dad was taking a bath so I was trying to hurry before he came back in the room to watch the ten o'clock news. My mom was gone to bed already, she went to bed early every night. She heard me saying, I knew he had lied so she told me to dial the number again. I said Daddy is going to catch me." She said, "You are a grown woman and this person might be your husband so call him back right now!"

All of my sisters and brothers were on their own now except my baby sister but she's away in college. I guess my mama had put in all of her years with us and was ready for us all to leave. Well, I dialed the phone again and he answered. We talked until my daddy came in the room. Surprisingly, even to myself I told my dad about him and asked his opinion. Now, I promise you my dad went to the third grade, but he was one of the smartest, wisest men I have ever known, both then and until he died several years ago.

"Well, you say you prayed for a husband and it's no way he could have heard you in Houston, Texas. He said he prayed for a wife and I don't know a lot about God but I do know a lot about prayer, just keep talking to him and time will tell!"

Was this my dad, the mean strict man that I had grown up around? He could be as mean as a bear or as gentle as a lamb. I went to bed feeling so good that night. Everything was perfect I knew God had answered my prayer. The best part was my parents were okay with it. Their opinion meant the world to me. There were just two more people I had to tell that response probably would help me to decide to continue talking to him. I had such a deep close relationship with both of them. I was so close to my oldest sister. I guess I tried to be her protector I don't know. Even today I'd sometimes rather go through rough times than for her to have to suffer anything. I guess I think I'm a tough cookie.

I got to see her every Friday and unless I was working on Saturday, I'd spend the night with her, we would sleep on the floor in the living room, we could not be separated, and the next day we would get the kids dressed and we would shop until we dropped. When I told her the news she knew him and was very happy for me. The next person was my best friend in the whole world, Jean. We were church buddies, I helped her with her shopping, when her son was diagnosed with cancer, he was younger than me; I went to the city with her for his chemo treatments. Jean loved him dearly and hated to see him in pain, so I stayed in the room with him to get his treatments and on the long trip back home he'd be so sick until I would sit on the back seat and let him lay his head on my lap and sleep. He died within a year at age eighteen.

I waited until Sunday on the way to church and broke the news to her. She said well you know you prayed and God answered you. I was so glad she understood.

The phone calls kept coming and I began to really enjoy talking to him. Sometimes we'd be on the phone for three hours. I loved how spiritual he was. He was not boring at all. He taught me so much about the bible. I loved learning the word and for the first time in my life I was really beginning to understand God's word. He was a dynamic bible teacher.

After church one Sunday evening Jean took me home and everyone was gone. She knew I hated being home alone (I still do) so she waited with me. I fixed us a big plate of food that my mom had cooked. Soon the phone rang, it was him. This was about a month or so after he called me at the store the first time. He asked all of his usual questions, "How is the Lord treating you?" "Just great," I replied each time. "Well, how are you treating the Lord?" "I'm doing my best to give him the best of my service," was my reply. We went on to talk about how church was for the day and so on. I noticed he was different today, there was a sense of strangeness, and it was as if he was holding back in the conversation. I kept asking was something wrong but he assured me it wasn't. Finally, he said, "I'm getting married," my heart dropped to the bottom of my stomach, I was hurt, disappointed and devastated. But I played it off well.

"Congratulations!" "Wait a minute you haven't even asked me whom I'm marrying and you congratulating me. It's you; you and I are getting married. I will be home for Thanksgiving and I'm bringing the ring with me."

"What? You just can't say we'll getting married you have to ask me, I might say no."

At the time I thought he was a man of great unwavering faith, years later I would think differently.

I told Jean he said we are getting married, she said, I don't care what he said, but about what you are going to say. I said you have to ask me. So he did and without any doubt, no hesitation, and no maybe's, I said yes. Jean and I kept this to ourselves for a few weeks. I was so happy but I could not tell anyone else until I was absolutely sure this was real. A few days before Thanksgiving he told me he could not come home after all because he was cutting his hair and cut a dash in it and had to shave his head bald. He did not want to meet my parents for the first time with an unattractive bald head. He decided to come home for Christmas. He called me twice every day and I would be so concerned about how much his phone bill was going to be. His bill was running between five and six hundred dollars a month but he didn't care because he made more than that a week.

I knew that I was going to marry him someday but something was wrong, I had not fallen in love with him, I just loved him.

I had only seen him two or three times so we were getting to know one another over the phone. He would tell me he loved me all the time but for the most part I could not say that to him. I had a love for him but I didn't know if it was the right love. However what I felt was a pretty good feeling.

Well, finally, it was Christmas week and he came home. I'm thinking he made it home late Saturday night. We made arrangements for him to come to my house Sunday evening around seven o'clock. It turned into a family event; we had fried fish and all the trimmings. A few minutes pass seven he arrived. Every head in the house was looking out a window or out the door. I heard comments from everywhere within a minute. It only takes a few seconds for my family to sum you up. Within a second we see you from head to toe. By this time I was shaking all over, I opened the door there he stood, still almost bald headed, he was well groomed, everything but his unpolished, un-shined shoes. My Aunt pointed that out when he left. We ate supper and went in the living room, everyone followed, we did not have one minute of alone time. Yet, I was so excited, I could not quit looking at him, he's the man from the phone, the man I'm going to marry this is really him. He spent the whole night talking to my family. I was glad because I was so shame faced until I probably would have been sitting there not saying a word. Things would change the next day with me, that evening he took me home, finally I got to ride in the beautiful car with the soft leather seats. It was great! When we arrived home we ate dinner, sat in the living room, alone this time and talked a long time. The next day I was off work so he came to the house early and my mom, Aunt, and I fixed dinner. He could not believe how well the food tasted. We had fried chicken, corn bread, collard greens, sweet potatoes, and mixed vegetable with ground beef and melted cheese (I fixed the mixed vegetables) so of course he said it was the best, however he ate thirds of mama's collard greens. No one could cook like Mama and Aunt. He washed his food down with several glasses of cold tea.

We talked, had a bible class for a couple hours, we did this each day, some nights my mom and dad would request we come in the family room so they could join in.

The next day after he brought me home from work we went on our first official date. It actually happened by coincident, the phone rang. It was my baby brother who was living in an apartment in at the time. He was cooking a rabbit and wanted my mom to make some biscuits for him. Betty Crocker couldn't beat her biscuits. She made the biscuits and asked us if we would take them to him. We agreed. He asked my dad would it be okay to take me to Pizza Hut. He said it would be fine.

My first secret is revealed. We took my brother his biscuits; we sat talked with him for about an hour before leaving. As we were leaving he noticed a complex where he said an ex-girlfriend of his use to live at while teaching uptown. I don't know if thinking of her made him do this or not, they had been apart for about a year or two. He stopped the car, leaned over to where I was sitting and attempted to kiss me. I was scared, before I knew it tears was rolling down my face. We had discussed this many times and I desperately wanted my first kiss to be on my wedding night. He told me he loved me and gave me a short sweet kiss. We left and went to Pizza Hut and left for home. As we entered back into my hometown above my home church cemetery I asked him to play his Al Green greatest gospel hit 8-track. He pulled over on the side of the road, put the tape in and said I thought you might like this to, so he kissed me very passionately. It was a decent kiss but for me I felt dirty, I thought my walk with Christ was diminished, I felt terrible. He assured me it was not a sin to kiss but I was not convinced. Christmas came and he spent most of the day with me. We did not exchange gifts. The days passed and we spent all the time we could to get to know one another. I was beginning to feel closer and closer to him and I was hoping he was too. Christmas passed and he still had not shown me the ring.

Well, by now I had told my family he was going to properly propose and give me the ring, I was both embarrassed and disappointed. It was now New Year's Eve a few hours before January 1982. My brother was preaching at a watch meet that night which would end before 12 a.m. I asked him to attend with me and he agreed. I wanted to look especially beautiful on this night. I had a very low self-esteem so it was hard to convince me I ever looked nice, I still deal with some of those issues even today.

My sister-in-law spent hours doing my hair; I wore a beautiful gray blazer, a wraparound red and gray plaid skirt, a red bowtie blouse and red shoes. My family went on and on about how beautiful I looked. I had coal black shiny hair that reached half way my back.

Finally, he arrived. I was waiting for him to tell me how beautiful I looked, he had never said I looked nice to him as a matter of fact I didn't know what he thought of my looks.

A second secret occurred, before we made it to the church he said I use to date a girl at the church we are going to and he said her relatives would all be there that night. He said I don't like what you are wearing and you must change your hair. I told him I could not because of all the time my sister in law spent fixing my hair. He didn't care he just wanted it different than it was. I gave in and combed my hair 2 or 3 times trying to please him, finally he chose a style he liked and that's the way I wore it.

When we made it to the church everyone asked why I changed my hair. I played it off somehow and they did not mention it again. Already I was beginning to learn to cover things up. If I had not given in maybe my destiny would have been different. It was a test, a sick minded test.

On the way home, he stopped on the middle of an old country gravel road, under the moonlight and stars, he said, "It's a good thing you changed your hair or this would not be happening. If you had not done as I told you....He opened the glove compartment and took out a jewelry box. I was nervous, confused, disappointed, and yet happy. He opened the box the ring was absolutely beautiful, he slipped it on my hand and asked me to marry him; I said yes I'll marry you.

I know what you are thinking; signs were there you should have taken notice. When you want something to be so right you cover up signs, you ignore them, and that's what I did time after time. I ignored the kiss, I ignored him making me change my hair, and I just wanted to be married. I was in too deep now to get out. Everyone was expecting me to get married. When we arrived home everyone waited up for us, I stood under the light as he asked my daddy's permission to marry me. He said yes then I showed off the ring. Everyone was amazed, it was absolutely beautiful. This was supposedly the happiest night of my life. However the hair incident lingered in the back of my mind. The next day or two he went back to Houston, Texas. I missed him so much. We continued talking on the phone. He wanted to get married in February but I did not want a quick wedding, I needed some time to plan a big wedding. My oldest sister would not have had it any other way. I think I was the first person in my community to have a real beautiful church wedding. We set the date it would be April 4, 1982 at 4:00p.m.

CHAPTER 2

THE ENGAGEMENT

I CONTINUED TO WORK AT the local dollar store. Word spread that the virgin was getting married. I was known over the city for being a virgin and a Christian young lady. I was proud of this fact, proud that I had preserved myself; I knew fornication was wrong and I wanted no part of it.

My baby sister was still away in college, she would come some weekends. I chose my oldest sister as my matron of honor, my youngest sister, and all of my sister in laws as maids of honor. My nephew was ring bearer and both of my nieces were flower girls and junior brides. All of my brothers and brothers in law were groomsmen. He chose a friend as his best man.

My oldest sister and I chose the wedding colors mauve and burgundy.

Jean and I continued all of the things we'd been doing as far as church was concerned.

One night during revival the young man Jean had wanted me to marry came and begged me to change my mind and marry him, we talked and hour but in the end the answer was still no.

A young man that no one knew was interested in me came on my job one day and cried regretting that he had been to bashful to ask me out, secretly I knew he liked me and ironically I kind of liked him too, he later married one of my best friends.

The next few months was about getting dresses made, renting tuxedos, getting a menu together, and being busy, busy.

Believe it or not I did not have to spend a dime, everyone agreed to buy their own fabric for dresses, everyone paid for their own tuxedos, I used the Methodist church which was much bigger than my church and it was free. The newspaper ran my announcement for free, and fortunately the man who owned the florist was one of our best customers so because of being so nice to him he agreed to do all my decorations which included everything for free. The only thing left was the wedding cake and the photographer. Again one of my customers was a professional photographer and he did all my pictures for free and choreographed my wedding as well.

The wedding cake was a big decision for me, my brother wanted a lady from our community to make it but another older lady who was a good friend of mine, very Christian hearted asked to do it. We decided to let my friend make it.

Well, the days seemed to be going by faster and faster. The wedding date was approaching. My oldest sister and I continued shopping almost on a daily basis. We were both full of joy and excitement.

The wedding gifts began rolling in weeks before the wedding. Mama's living room was being overtaken with beautifully wrapped gifts.

We took a day to look for the nightgown I would wear on my wedding night. That was one decision I wanted to make on my own. I wonder if my oldest sister would remember all these things. We went from store to store and finally, there it was, THE PERFECT GOWN.

I did not want anything real revealing or sexy. I wanted something that was feminine, modest, and befitting to a virgin. This gown did not take away the nervousness I had about this night, but I knew that it was absolutely perfect. I knew that I would be shaking like a leaf on a tree on my wedding night.

It was cut above the knee, a low cut neckline with spaghetti straps; it was made of fine silk. The robe was made of organza and was a tad bit below the knee. It was my size this was made just for me on my special night. Little did I know that I would only have it on for a few minutes. You will read about this in the **next chapter**.

Well, the day finally arrived when my oldest sister and I went shopping for the perfect matron of honor's dress and my wedding dress and shoes. Her dress was more than beautiful. Burgundy long to the floor, it was silk with a hat to match, it looked like something from the 30's. When she tried on her dress and came out she looked like someone out of the movies. She was gorgeous and she knew it. My oldest and youngest sisters both had such confidence; they were beautiful young ladies and did not allow anyone to make them feel differently. We had my oldest sisters dress so now it was my time.

We drove across town to J.C. Penny's to look in their catalog. My heart was beating out of control with anticipation. There we both sat looking in books when the perfect dress appeared before my eyes. It was nothing like the dresses of today but it was more than beautiful for the 80's. It had long lace sleeves with a lace bodice front that would fit tight in the waist and flare out with a long trail. I did not need a veil because my sister in law wanted so much for me to wear her veil; she saved me the time and effort of looking for one.

We placed the order for the dress and I'm not sure about the original price but the sales lady said to just bring back a hundred dollars and the dress is yours. God was just continuing to work things out for me. We ate lunch and went home.

I told mama about the dress and asked her to talk to my daddy about the cost and everything. Later that night she told him how much the wedding dress was going to cost. I had no doubt, I was sure that for a man that carried two wallets with enough hundred dollar bills to choke a horse he would just go in his rubber band and reach me a Benjamin Franklin. I could not have been more wrong. He fussed, cussed, and acted a fool as he would do to me quite often. I never understood why he had such wrath toward me at times but I guess some things are not meant to be known.

It was about two weeks before the big day and I had no dress and no money. My oldest sister was all spent out or she would have bought it. I didn't want to ask my brothers because they had to rent their own tuxedos. What was I going to do? My sister in law suggested asking my groom. I would have almost rather called off the wedding than to do that but I did. He did not hesitate. I will put it in the mail tomorrow. I received it in the mail the next day and went got the dress.

My next problem was how I was going to get my shoes. My mom said, don't worry that's one thing your cheap ass daddy is going to get. One thing about mama, she was one of the most honest-respectable women I've ever known and was meek and quiet always but when she had to make a stand she would. She took Daddy in the room, I didn't hear a word she said but in a few minutes he walked out and reached me two twenties and a ten. "Here, take this I want to buy your wedding shoes."

I wanted to laugh so hard but I knew not to press my luck.

Saturday night a week before the wedding, my oldest sister, youngest sister, and her boyfriend took me out to dinner, it was sort of a private engagement party. We went to the Half Shell which was a seafood restaurant. Seafood is my favorite of all foods and whoever was in the back cooking sure knew what they were doing. The food was perfect. Everything was so good. We had a blast and I guess we made it back home around 12:30 or 1:00a.m.

We had already taken my sisters boyfriend home and went in room to lie across the bed and we talked until we fell asleep. This would be the night my oldest sister would tell me what to expect on my wedding night.

However, mama and daddy said, "he has been calling you all night and we really believe he's mad as hell." "We told him you were at dinner with your sisters but he really didn't believe us."

Actually, I thought nothing of it but I went ahead and called him anyway.

He said, "You know that other lying girl I was involved with was running around lying, sleeping with men, telling me she was out with family when I would call her 2 and 3 in the morning and she wasn't home. Baby, The Wedding is OFF! Don't you ever call me again and I sure won't be calling you. You don't know how angry I am. I guess you are no good just like the rest of them."

There I was trying to explain that I was being honest. "I was with my family, we only went to dinner, please, don't call the wedding off, I promise I want go anywhere again."

"I guess you be lying on Sunday's too when you come home late and say you been at church all day. You know what, I'm sorry you put the wedding announcement in the paper and I'm sorry you'll be embarrassed but the wedding is off."

Little did I know that this was about control, about manipulation about training me for the future. It was one thing I was sure about it would be a secret I would forever keep I would find something to say about why I cancelled the wedding but it would not be because I had dinner with my sisters.

My sisters was calling for me when they heard me hang up. I told them to wait a minute I'd be right there. I tried to call him back; I would beg him and plead with him to not cancel the wedding. He took his phone off the hook. There I sat crying, heartbroken and molding myself into the person I would become in the future. I could hear my mom and dad snoring so I knew they couldn't hear me crying. How would I face my sisters, they would see my eyes, they would know something was wrong. Somehow I gathered the strength to get off the sofa, my feet felt as if I had on concrete shoes but I managed to make it to the room. The lights were off, only the moonlight gleamed through my youngest sisters lace curtains.

They never noticed I had been crying. There it was another secret successfully concealed.

I don't know how I did it but it would become a regular part of my life acting as if everything was perfect in my life. Sometimes my life would be falling apart and no one knew.

I had fun, my oldest sister screaming with her sex stories. I never knew my oldest sister knew so much. I guess her husband had taught her a lot. The funniest thing that happened that night was when my baby sister didn't know where the man inserted himself into the woman. She was extremely confused. Even I knew that! Hours later they fell asleep, I guess around 3:00 am. I quietly got up and called him. He still would not answer the phone. I lay my head on the arm of the sofa and cried myself to sleep.

Every sign every action was telling me I might be making a mistake. I promise you God does not let things sneak upon you. If you pay attention, he will show you things.

I woke up early Sunday morning and carried out my usual routine. My brother picked me up for Sunday school and Jean picked me up for church. Of course I tried calling him but there was still no answer. At 6:30 pm I was to be at my home church for a wedding shower. I didn't know what to do, should I make the announcement at the church that the wedding was off. I was literally a ball of nerves. My stomach felt like I had eaten rocks for dinner. I went ahead and got dressed. Just as we were all ready to leave for the church someone drove up and blew their horn. I looked out the glass door, it was him! I ran outside, we threw our arms around one another both apologizing at the same time.

I guess right then I was the happiest person in the state of Mississippi. The shower was great; it turned into a church service.

Everyone was crying, I was a great attribute to my church and although they knew I had to begin my own life they really hated to see me go.

After the shower we came home and spent some time together. Neither he nor I mentioned what had happened the night before. This was the beginning of having a problem and not talking it out or discussing it. I should have talked to him and let him knew what my family meant to me. We had grown up very close to one another. We grew up where we really did not hear a lot of arguing out of our parents. My mom said that they had disagreements like all married people but they tried not to discuss things in front of their children.

Our daddy never hit our mama but I would learn later that the situation was different in his home. He lived in a violent home where there was no trust and not much love. I will not discuss this issue in the book to protect his family image and to protect myself against a lawsuit. However, you will plainly see the effects your home life can have on you, both the good and the bad.

Monday morning came and he was at my house around 7:00 am. We arrived at the hospital very early to get our blood test and later we went to purchase the marriage certificate.

I had kept some things within myself for several weeks hoping he would be honest and tell me about them.

My oldest brother and my brother-in-law asked me one day did I know he had two children and that he had been engaged to each child's mother. I was very embarrassed to admit that I wasn't aware of it.

Well, here we are about five or six days from being married and we have this big secret.

There was no way to do it but point blank ask him. "Do you have any children?" I asked.

"Yes, I have an eight year old son. His mom is ……….. We were engaged to be married but she would not become a Christian so I could not marry her. She had the whole wedding planned but I did not show up at the church. I had explained to her I wasn't coming."

Somehow I understood what he felt because I too would not have married someone who wasn't a Christian.

"I might have a three year old daughter, I'm not sure if she's mine." He explained his doubts and I cannot go into an explanation but he had a good reason to doubt her.

However, his decision to not marry her had nothing to do with the baby it was because of a difference in religious beliefs. She had been coming on my job flouncing herself and the little girl in front of me for weeks before I knew who she was.

His Mom had fixed lunch for us so we went by her house before going back to my home. This entire week would become a living nightmare for me. A hold host of events would take place that will probably even today put my family in a state of shock. Things happened that I've kept inside of me for twenty-three years. It's time to tell, it's time to help some of you young ladies and young men out there in a situation that you need to get out of.

She served fried chicken, fried corn, mashed potatoes and gravy and strawberry Kool-Aid. I wasn't very hungry so he ate his food and most of mine. She was the only person home. And she soon left for the laundry mat.

Something didn't feel right. I saw the washer and dryer so why was she leaving. When she left he asked me to come in the bedroom and help him get his things unpacked. I refused I told him to bring his things in the living room and we would unpack them there. He got angry, very angry, and said forget it. We'll just sit here on the sofa and watch television. I asked him to take me home, I'm not comfortable being here in the house alone with you.

He leaned over and started to kiss me. He even kissed me on my neck leaving a hickey the size of a quarter. I kept asking him to please stop but it was apparent that NO was not in his vocabulary. Before I knew it he stood in front of me, exposed himself an asked me to perform oral sex on him. He tried to force himself in my mouth, it made me gag. I kept pushing him away until he finally gave up. He stood in front of me and masturbated. I had never seen anything like this in my life. I was totally shaken. The results of this spilled on my clothes. He cleaned himself up, brought in a wet towel and proceeded to try and clean my clothes. We left after that. All the way home I could not look at him or talk to him, I went home and immediately changed clothes, hoping my mom and Aunt wouldn't notice anything. By this time Mom had dinner ready for us so we ate dinner and from there we sat out on the porch and talked to Mama and my Aunt.

Later on in the evening my brother came, he saw what I had been hiding all the day long, he saw the hickey on my neck. All day I had hung my hair over my shoulder and managed to hide it from my mom.

I was passed embarrassed. My brothers would have never expected me to let things get out of hand. I blamed myself although I had repeatedly asked him to stop. It was not something I wanted. I did not want to see him expose himself neither. I guess he felt he had gone too far so he left around six or seven pm to visit his sick grandfather. I wanted so much to tell what he had done but again I feared the embarrassment of the wedding being called off. I kept this secret, you are the first besides he and I to know what happened.

The next day he came by my job and picked me up for lunch. He decided to just ride around the city for a while. He parked on the side of the bypass to talk. That ended in him asking for a kiss, I absolutely refused. I thought what had happened the day before might happen again. After at least an hour of asking for a kiss he became noticeably angry and drove away. We went up on a street called Hwy 33, he tried again, this time grabbing my head over as if to force me to kiss him against my will. I will not kiss you I repeatedly said. You promised me all these things could wait until we were married.

I guess some of you might think I was being unreasonable. I had my rights and my beliefs and I just was not comfortable kissing him. Actually we were parked within a half block of my brother's house. I told him not to touch me again or I would run to his house and tell. He cranked the car and drove away. I told him to take me back to work because I was already two hours late. "You will get there when I take you there, you should just go on and quit anyway."

I took my comb from my purse to straighten my hair. I opened the mirror in his car and began combing it. He asked to see the comb to do his hair but I said I'm using it. I would give it to him as soon as I finished my own hair. He was already furious so this wasn't good enough. He snatched it out of my hair demanding to see it now. I gave in, I did not argue with him it was just a comb!

To him it was control. I had given him many reasons to know he could push me over as he pleased, so things would only excel for the worse. I should have told him immediately about his attitude but I was too good, too sweet to hurt anyone's feelings. Actually, I was a naive coward who thought being spiritual meant turning the other cheek in spite of how it made me feel. That's anything but spiritual it is not God's will for anyone to mistreat a person.

Even that day he had fussed about the outfit I had worn. It was truck day at the store and I would be unpacking boxes all day. I had worn a camouflage shirt with an olive green skirt. I always wore this outfit to disguise the dust and dirt from the boxes.

My explanation was not good enough, he said, "I have friends, ex-girlfriends, and family coming in this store all the time and what you have on is an embarrassment to me."

In later chapters you will see how even what I wore was left up to him.

What you are doing now could very well determine your future in your relationship.

After returning back to work my boss called me into his office. He was a very attractive twenty-five year old. He was about 6'3", light skinned and well dressed. He admired me a lot both him and his beautiful wife. He did not like my fiancé at all. He's pushy, bossy, and does not fit you at all. You can do better he said. I don't like him, he's going to be trouble for you. Please don't marry him, he said I promise you he's not going to even let you watch television, you won't be able to fix your hair or dress like you want to. He's going to remodel your whole life.

He did not profess to be a Christian; he did not attend church often at all. How did he know, what did he see that let him know this. I laughed at Him jokingly telling him you hate to lose a good worker.

He assured me he knew what he was talking about, he said he has already tried to make you do things you didn't want to do. Tears was rolling down his face, he was pleading with me. I knew in my heart he was right.

"Shirley, I promise you if you marry him, I'm quitting my job, I'm going to take my wife and move from this city, when news arrive here of how he's treating you I want to be far enough away that I can't hear it. I will hurt him if he ever hurts you."

He said he loved me because I was the first person that he had ever known that really acted like a Christian and lived like one.

The people in that community thought the world of me. I had genuine love from so many people and I can't think of any person I ever mistreated.

I loved loving people and I loved being loved. Even today my children tell me I try to find good in a roach.

I knew there was a lot of good in my fiancé, I saw controlling mean streaks in him but I could change all that. I was going to treat him so nice, love him so much, pray with him and every little mean streak would just magically disappear.

I was fooling myself. He picked me up from work that evening and he was as sweet as potato pie the rest of the night. We sat and talked to he fell asleep on my shoulder. He was like a newborn sleeping baby. He was so innocent, so sweet, he was perfect. He can be this way always but what I failed to remember was that he was going to wake up.

When he left I sat down and had a father-daughter talk. I had not had many of these before. Ever since I had become a Christian my dad stayed his distance from me and if we had any conversations in the pass, it was normally him cussing me out and me arguing back asking him why he was mistreating me. You know it is so odd, if l knew my dad was accusing me of something wrong, I would stand right up to him to defend myself. However, years later I'll become one of the biggest wimps you'll ever meet.

I asked my dad what you really think of him. I respected my daddy's opinion so much. I believe I was hoping he would tell me to stay the hell away from him. I promise you I had never known my daddy to be wrong about a person's character. He could read people and see through them but he could not read a book. When he said in his deep country voice "I tell ya one thang," it was time to sit back and listen and learn.

"I tell ya one thang," he said. He would always call him by his first and last name. "_____ _____ is a good man, a hardworking man and he'll be a good husband as long as you walk the straight line."

"The straight line, what you mean," I asked.

"As long as you do everything he wants you to, the way he want you to, when he wants you too, you'll get along just perfect with him! If you ever do things your way, you'll suffer the consequences."

I went on to bed thinking about what he said. That will be easy I plan to be a wife that obeys and do everything to please my husband anyway. Piece of cake! On the other hand, Dad probably went to bed thinking she's headed for a life filled with hell.

The next day I was at work, in the back of the store folding towels when he came in. I gave him a quick hug. We talked for a while and then he asked me a question that stopped me dead in my tracks.

"Shirley, can we go to the hotel tonight?" he asked.

"For what?," I said very stupidly.

"I just want to be alone with you. Just hold you in my arms and talk. We never really have time alone, your family is always there always walking in and out the room. I promise you I won't try anything," he said.

He was so sincere, so loving so kind. I said no way, I can't do it, and I just can't. We argued about this about 30 minutes.

"The wedding is off, baby! And this time I mean it. I'm tired of you; you are boring and no fun at all! It's off. I'm going home, packing my clothes and going back to Houston." This was around 10:30a.m. He stormed out and left. There I stood again, the Friday before my wedding and my groom had just walked out. I didn't try calling him or anything I just literally gave up. I did not cry, I didn't call anyone I just accepted that I would not be getting married.

What kind of preacher is he anyway, how could he expect me to sleep with him two days before the wedding?

The hours passed by as slow as molasses on a cold day. Each hour the pain worsened. I could only imagine all the gossip, having to return people gifts and all the money my family had spent.

On Fridays my brother would always stop by the store to see if I needed a ride home. Well six o'clock finally rolled around and my brother drove up and waited outside.

Just as he drove up I noticed another vehicle drive up as well. It was him, my fiancé; he had not left after all. I was happy, relieved and overjoyed to see him. I got in the car; we did not talk about what had happened earlier in the day. We just listened to gospel music all the way home.

When we went inside the house he asked my daddy would it be okay for us to go to Pizza Hut. He said yes. I took a bath, got dressed and we left around seven thirty or eight. We went to Pizza

Hut, everything was kind of quiet between the two of us. What made him decide to stay-a million thoughts were running through my mind.

He looked into my eyes and told me he loved me. I responded with the same answer. I did love him but I later learned I was not in love with him.

I asked him to take his glasses off, he had the most beautiful brown eyes, with long wonderful eyelashes. His eyes fascinated me and I loved looking into them. We sat there and talked for hours when finally he suggested something that would change me drastically.

He wanted to go to the hotel next door. I insisted that we should just leave and go home but he would not take no for an answer. He assured me we were only going to talk. A part of me knew not to trust him but then another part of me wanted him to be the honest, loving, spiritual preacher that I had believed him to be.

We arrived at the hotel he went in the office and paid for a room. I had not ever been to a hotel before, I knew not what to expect. He drove up to our room, I literally froze in my seat. I was pleading and begging, please take me home. I just want to go home. Every negative thought in the world was in my head. Your daddy told you he might end up raping or killing you. I imagined being thrown in the woods somewhere.

He kept saying get out of the car because I am not going to leave. I managed to get out the car and went in the room and sat at the table which was placed in front of the window.

He tried to comfort me by saying I promise I'm not going to try anything, I just want to talk. I had not ever been so nervous in my entire life. I was trembling, words had a problem coming out my mouth, and I felt as if though I had swallowed a whole apple.

He pulled off his shoes and blazer and sat on the side of the bed. He said, "I've been hearing some rumors that you were having an affair with the preacher you follow every Sunday."

I tried so much to assure him this was not true. This preacher was like an ideal father to me I loved him with all my heart and the closest he had ever been to me was to hug me and kiss me on the cheek, like a father would his daughter. I too had heard these rumors many times but I never let it get to me, for I knew the truth.

I was a virgin, I was proud of the fact that he would be my first on our wedding night. From the time I knew what sex was I knew I would be like my mama I would wait for marriage. This was something sacred and holy to me.

"My brother told me there are no virgins left in this world. He said you are just lying to get me. He said I would be a fool to marry you and not be sure whether you are a virgin or not. I'm not going to hurt you but I do have to know or there won't be a wedding."

"I promise you I'm a virgin, I have never let a person even touch me before. I love God and I know what his word says about fornication. You'll see two days from now. Please, trust me. I'm not like the other girls you were with. My family will tell you about me. I love you but you can't do this to me. I'm leaving, I'll call my sister to come and get me. I'm scared."

I stood up and walked toward the door. I reached to unlock the door and remove the chain. He grabbed my hand, "I'm not going to hurt you. I promise you baby." By now I'm crying up a storm, things are out of control. He asked me to sit on the bed, I refused. He pulled me over and told me to lie down. I did. He pulled off his clothes. I was still dressed. He tried unsuccessfully to get my underclothes down. I had such a grip until he couldn't budge me.

I usually did not wear a girdle but I was more than glad I did that night. He laid on top of me and tried to insert himself inside of me anyway. Just as he touched me with his private part blood poured down. He did not insert himself.

I felt nasty, dirty, and filthy that he had touched his penis to me and we were not married.

He jumped up. "Oh my God! Oh my God Shirley! What have I done? I am so sorry. Please forgive me. I should have believed you. I'm sorry for touching you like that. Please don't tell anyone. I have never been so sorry for anything in my whole life." He put his clothes back on while I went to the restroom to clean myself up. I felt so weird, strange, and unclean. What was going on?! I truly didn't understand all what had just happened. I was clear that we didn't have sex but unclear about why he didn't believe me. I came out the restroom still crying uncontrollably. He tried to hug me but I assured him if he touched me again I would scream.

As odd as this sound I could tell that he really was sorry. It is so strange how Satan uses others to cause pain on God's children.

His growing up with unfaithful women and dating unfaithful women had caused me a night of terror. His mind was vexed and controlled with doubt that no lady could be honest.

In spite of any of this I should have called the police. I should have told someone but instead I held another secret. As secret that protected him. Again, I was more concerned about his feeling than my own. Although, he definitely did not insert himself there's a word now for what he did, it's called date rape. I was so devastated until on the way home we got lost and ended up in another city. I guess we arrived home around two a.m.

I learned years later that my daddy and my brother was so worried until they came looking for us.

On the next morning I didn't know how to act. The bleeding had stopped. I took a bath and got dressed. He came early that morning. We ate breakfast and just sat around and talked most of the day. We did not talk about what happened the night before. As a matter of fact I buried this secret and thought I would never dig it up. However, you or someone you know needs to know this was wrong. If a person says no, they mean NO! You never have a right to go beyond what a person want and desire. This should be a decision on both parts. Although he was sorry and begged me to marry him that night to wrong his right, it was too little too late. I still was determined to marry him on the next day which would be Sunday. I also knew that I would not let his mistake mess up our wedding night.

This time was unlike any of the other things he had said or done. Somehow, I felt so sorry for him, thinking how a mother could have done so many things that her son, her child could not trust any ladies at all. She had fixed his mind for life and I knew that God would ultimately be the one who would have to help him. Yet, I was thinking, I'll be so perfect, such a good wife that he'll have no choice but to trust me.

I was fooling myself but somehow I had trained myself to believe if I tried to be good it would make others be the same way. If someone hit me I didn't hit them back because I thought it would make them not fight, all it caused was me to get beat up quite often.

I couldn't change him only God could.

Today is the day of my biggest wedding reception. We had wedding rehearsal at the church. Everything went well and before we knew it we were back at Mama's house.

The church had given me a shower, so had my sister-in-law at her house, friends had brought gifts by the house and by my job.

Money inside of cards was piled on the table. My family gave me the final shower along with the rehearsal dinner.

His sister and niece were in the wedding so he brought them over for dinner. We had a blast. We had fried catfish with all the trimmings. He swallowed a bone but after my mom filled him up with bread and vinegar it went away. He knew that by tradition he would have to leave before 12:00am because the groom wasn't supposed to see the bride on the wedding day. He gave me a hug and we said good night. I was so excited until it was hard for me to get to sleep. My sisters and I talked most of the night until we all finally fell asleep. I'm sure I was the last one to fall asleep.

CHAPTER 3

THE WEDDING

WELL, THIS IS THE BIG day, the morning had finally arrived. Mama woke me and my sisters up around eight o'clock a.m.

I felt really weird not getting dressed for church. We all had a head full of rollers, nightgowns and slippers. Already I was starting to be a bundle of nerves. We started getting nieces and nephews fed and bathed.

I didn't eat anything. I was so nervous I doubt if it would have stayed down anyway.

I combed two of my niece's hair who would be participating in the wedding. The hours seemed to pass by quickly.

The wedding was scheduled to begin at four o'clock p.m. The church had been decorated the day before so we didn't have to be concerned about that.

All my family started arriving. Everyone looked absolutely stunning. The males dressed in burgundy tux with mauve shirts and the females in beautiful mauve dresses with floral chiffon shawls.

The flower girls and the junior brides were absolutely breathtaking. They were beautiful walking dolls.

By now everyone is dressed my hair has been done. I have on my shoes and everything. My mama and daddy came out and although I'd seen my daddy dressed up many times it was something different about today. He looked so good in his tux, his hair was perfectly combed, and he was handsome. Mama was beautiful. She was perfect. My aunt was dressed like mama and so was the groom's mother. They looked like three southern bells.

Well, it's about three thirty. I slipped on mama's house coat. My oldest sister and others put my veil on my head and I very nervously headed for the car. I planned to put on my dress once I entered the church.

We loaded the vehicles with all the food and punch for the reception which would be at the church as well.

The only time we would line up our cars one behind the other was on sad occasions (funerals). This was a first joyous, happy following. We arrived at the church. I rushed into one of the rooms as to not be seen by anyone. The parking lot was already filling up.

The groom's family arrived shortly after us. They had brought food as well, so they all went into the kitchen and got everything spread out on the tables.

Soon after that my friend arrived with the cakes she very carefully set it up. The cake was absolutely beautiful. It was a three tier cake, white inside decorated with white icing and pink flowers.

It is a few minutes pass four, the preacher has arrived, all the participants in the wedding. It was time for everyone to line up as we had practiced the night before. However there is a major problem. The musician is playing the piano it was the groom and best man's cue to get in place but there was no groom. He was almost an hour late. His mom was trembling with fear, she was so afraid he was standing me up as he had done the two other girls before. She said he'd left long before them and should have arrived at the church before them.

I don't know how I did it but I remained calm. My mother whom had already been seated in the church came to ask what was going on. The whole wedding party was nervous. I told her he was running a few minutes late but assured her he was coming.

A few minutes before five, he walked in the church with no explanation. Everyone was asking him why was he late but he avoided answering them by laughing. He later told me he had gone to visit his son on the way to the church. He had cried and threw a tantrum because he didn't want his daddy to marry me. He stayed to try to comfort him and stop him from crying. I thought then that would always be a problem in our marriage but in all honesty it was not.

The ushers lit the candles turned the lights off and the wedding finally began.

Everyone marched in as they had practiced. My dad and I stood in the doorway of our room watching everyone as they walked in. Soon it was only my two nieces left, there they stood with their rose pedals in little white baskets, dressed in beautiful white miniature wedding dresses. The ushers rolled out the carpet and they walked in. The musician began playing, "Here comes the bride."

My daddy took me by my hand. We were both shaking furiously. "Well, I guess it's our turn," he said. We slowly walked down the aisle I was leaving one daddy in a sense to marry another one.

The preacher asked, "Who gives this bride to be wed in holy matrimony?"

"I do," said my dad.

We had a prayer by a preacher and the soloist sung two songs. She sang "Oh How I Love Jesus," and "The Lord's Prayer."

We held hands the whole time, he was trembling badly as he stood their dressed all in white. He was very handsome in his long tailed tux. He told me some years later he stood there thinking I was the worse looking lady who walked down the aisle. It was not a joke, he really felt that way and that hurt me for years but I'm over it now.

We exchanged vows, kissed, and were pronounced man and wife. It felt good. I had a new last name.

We took pictures for the wedding album and proceeded to the reception. We cut the cake and soon after that he went outside to greet his guest. My sister helped me to change into my after the wedding dress. It was a beautiful two piece white outfit that she had made for me.

I felt as beautiful in it as I did in my wedding dress. However, I wasn't feeling happy, my groom wasn't by my side. He was outside talking while I got stuck inside serving wedding cake. My ushers reserved the top layer of my wedding cake which was to be eaten on our first year anniversary. Actually, it ended up staying in my oldest sisters freezer three or four years until she finally threw it away. We were living out of state but thinking about it now she could have expressed it to us.

The ushers cleaned up everything and around eight o'clock we left the church. I only had one wedding bouquet so I didn't throw it; I just gave it to my sister-in-law, his sister that asked for it.

We all arrived back home around eight fifteen. I started getting my luggage and everything ready for the car. We were supposed to spend a week at a hotel before leaving for our home in Houston, Texas.

He called me in my room we sat on the bed he said I have something to tell you. "We are not going to the hotel; we are leaving for Houston tonight."

My heart was crushed. I was not ready for this. I was not prepared to leave for Houston yet. He explained it would be embarrassing to come back and face our families after the honeymoon. Nothing mattered what he said, I could not stop crying. I was more embarrassed to say to them we were leaving for Houston at nine or ten.

Their hearts were broken, how would we fit all my things in his car. He started loading the gifts on the back seat. Although, Lincolns are huge inside, they still had a hard time fitting things in. He only had a peep hole to see out the back window, things were stacked all the way to the roof of the car. We had to just squeeze all my shoes and clothes in the trunk. Soon, everything was packed and it was time to leave.

I had not been able to stop myself from crying. How can I do this, how can I leave my family. How could I leave Jean whom I said my good-byes to at the church, but I thought I would see her after the honeymoon.

Well this was it; there was not a straight face in the yard. My brothers were angry because of him rushing to leave. I think most of us thought he was being mean, controlling, and hateful. All the females were hurt but above all them my oldest sister was crushed the most. I hugged everyone. I started with mama and daddy. Everyone got a hug from the youngest to the oldest. I saved her for last. I knew she would be the hardest person to turn loose. She was living much of the life that was awaiting me. I had tried to be her protector, her shoulder to lean on, her sister, but more than anything her friend.

The family had to pull us apart. It was awful. I felt like if I went away she would give up all hope, who would push her to keep going.

Finally, I had to literally fall into the car, my legs and feet were not helping. I was numb, it's like a part of me died that night and to some extent I never recovered it. As we went up the road and got on the highway I could hear my oldest sister screaming. I could see mama and Aunt holding her. I pleaded with him to go back but he kept driving. You have to let your family go. I knew he was right but my sister needed me. I had always been there for her, even on the few occasions that my daddy whipped her. I would get on the floor locked around his leg begging him to stop. When her husband would hit her, I was sometimes there begging him to stop, insisting I would never go through the same thing.

We stopped in his hometown to say our good-byes as well. There was no shedding of tears there. I took a few minutes to call my mom and check on them. Everyone was still crying. We stayed with his family for a few minutes and then started on our eight hour trip to Texas. The time seemed to go by so slowly. We did not talk a lot just listened to music. I sat close by my door still thinking of my family I left behind and wondering what my new life would be like.

The roads were dark and long and as we entered the different cities my eyes were wide open with amazement. The bright lights the tall bridges, the interstates, the buildings were all new to a country girl who had never been farther than Mississippi.

The excitement of seeing so many new things helped ease my mind and allowed me to quit thinking so much of my family. As we were about to enter a small little town we were held up by a train. He asked me to slide over and I did. We sat there I guess about fifteen minutes, kissing the entire time. For the first time I was free to enjoy the pleasure of the kisses. It suddenly dawned on me, I'm married, I'm actually married and on the way to my new home. I was overjoyed.

Things seemed so right. I was nervous but I felt happy. When the train passed we drove off but this time was different, this time I sat as close to him as I could. I felt safe. The tears are now all gone and I could only think what the rest of the night would be like.

We began talking more; he would tell me a little history about each city we drove through. When we entered Lake Charles, Louisiana I was very afraid. The bridge was absolutely huge. All my life I was afraid of bridges. I would either close my eyes or get on the floor in the car so I wouldn't have to look at the water. This time was different I was scared, too scared not to look. We were up in the air it seemed. From a distance it seemed the bridge touched the sky. I think that night kind of broke my fear. Things have been different ever since. We had several more bridges to cross before finally entering the city limits of Houston. When we finally could see downtown Houston I was absolutely, downright amazed.

"Welcome home," he said, "Oh, we are finally here," I said.

The skyscrapers were just that, they seemed to reach the sky. There were thousands of lights shining from every side. My eyes were as big as the moon. I'm going to love this. I thought to myself. Although it was around five or six in the morning the freeways was packed with cars. I'm sure to most it was a pain in the neck, to me it was an adventure. After all I had never seen congested traffic before. Vehicles were lined up one behind the other in every lane. "You'll get use to this," he said.

We finally arrived in the area where he lived, it was called Spring Branch. Although we had grown up around whites all our lives and half my family was white. I was not prepared for my environment. There were hundreds of white faces, a few Mexicans and Indians, and almost no blacks. He assured me I would like living in this area because it was quiet and hardly any violence.

He drove to some apartments. The sign said Village Circle Apartments. He drove about midway the buildings and pulled into a parking spot. "We're home," he exclaimed. We got out of the car and walked toward our home. I was so nervous full of every imaginable thought. My main concern was how it is going to look. Finally, we were there, standing in front of the door, he hugged and kissed me and said welcome home.

I walked in. it was beautiful, warm, and very nicely decorated. It was perfect. The apartment consisted of a three piece red velvet living room suit with glass tables, separate kitchen, and dining room. We were both very tired so he said. I'll show you everything later, come this way to the bedroom. He turned the light on, the first thing I noticed was a quilt hanging over the window. He explained he used it to make the room dark during the day because he worked the graveyard shift. Then the bed caught my eyes and captivated me. It was red velvet, king size with a red velvet bed spread. It was probably the most beautiful bed I had ever seen in my life. I told him how beautiful everything was. We decided to freshen up before going to bed. I went first, locking the door behind me. I put on the lovely white night gown, combed my hair, sprayed on perfume and got into bed. I was shaking out of control. I was so afraid. He went in took a shower and came to bed. We laid there and talked trying our best to calm my nerves. He told me to lay my head on his chest so I did. I asked him to turn off the lights. He began caressing me. He assured me things would be slow and easy and he would not hurt me. I can honestly say although things was painful it was a beautiful experience. He was very gentle and patient. When I got up that morning I was bleeding. I called my mom to see what was going on, she told me not to worry it was happening because I was a virgin. This went on a week before stopping.

When he finally woke up, I asked if he wanted breakfast but after checking the cabinets and the refrigerator the only thing he had was a jar of grape jelly. He unloaded the car and we began the task of hanging all my clothes and putting away my shoes and purses. After finishing this I started opening the gifts, we had more of everything than we needed, so most of the stuff was stored away for later use. I saved all the cards for last and by the time I opened the last one we had a total over six hundred dollars. Only twenty of which had come from one of his friends.

I put the money away thinking it was mine to do as I wish. I would soon learn differently. He took all the trash outside and to the dumpster; we cleaned the floor and were done with all the unpacking before dark.

By now we were both very hungry and began discussing what we were going to eat. He decided to go for Long John Silver's seafood. He told me to stay home and he would go down the street and pick it up. Give me twenty dollars and I'll be right back. He was back in less than thirty minutes. The food was very good. When he came back, I had turned on the television and was sitting on the sofa. We went over to the table to eat, after which we sat back on the sofa. He said we needed to go over some things, some rules. I thought to myself "Rules!" I'm not a child. He explained that I could only watch the news and the gospel channel on television and that the radio was to remain on the station it was on and not to be moved. It was on the white gospel station. I was not use to anything he was expecting me to do. I was very discouraged and disappointed. The talk that I had with boss came to my mind, word for word. How could he have known, what did he know that I didn't know. I felt crushed because the one thing I enjoyed most was watching television. I made the mistake of not saying anything. I did not let him know I didn't want to abide by these rules. Within a few weeks this would really begin to weigh heavily on me. My days and nights were boring. I loved God with all my heart but I could not see why it was wrong to listen to black gospel or watch television. Another thing I was starting to notice was the fact he was asking for more and more of the money each day and that I was never allowed to go anywhere with him. He could go to different restaurants every day and bring the food home. I would get up each day and get dressed, hoping he would say come ride with me. Sunday came and I just knew we would attend church but he said he wasn't ready for everyone to meet me yet. I thought something is very strange about this but again I didn't ask for any explanations. Only time would tell why I did not go places with him.

The second and last week of our honeymoon was a little different. He said he was taking me to show me the city. The first day we did something fun, we went to the zoo. He was very displeased with what I wore but I thought I looked nice so I kept it on. I wore a navy skirt with a red bowtie blouse and a white shawl. My hair was very neatly combed. I would later find that it was my figure or the lack of having one that bothered him. Before marrying him I wrote him a long letter to inform him of some things. At that time I was at least forty pounds overweight, my stomach was not flat, my butt was flat and I sometimes had problems with my facial skin. He assured me that he loved me for whom I was. That was the understatement of the year.

I managed to ignore the fact that my clothes bothered him and enjoyed seeing all the animals, riding on the train, and seeing the children running and playing. I had only been to a zoo one other time so nothing was going to spoil my fun.

After seeing all the animals we went to the snack area to have lunch. The food was very good. We had cheeseburgers, fries, and coke. He took lots of pictures and after which we went home.

Our nights were compassionate and loving. Of course we spent a lot of time both day and night making love. My body was becoming adjusted and things were okay. In all of his bad ways when it comes to love making ninety percent of the time he was very kind, caring, and gentle.

The next day we went to one of his favorite places which was called Luby's Cafeteria, to eat. I was so embarrassed. I had never eaten at such a big place with so many people. He said for me not to worry he would show me what to do. We chose our food; fried chicken, macaroni-n-cheese, broccoli, greens, corn bread, and lemon pie. I had never eaten broccoli, I had never seen broccoli, but after tasting it covered with cheese, I loved it.

The day went well and we soon returned home. The next several days were adventurous as well. He taught me how to ride the metro bus just in case I would ever need to go someplace while he was at work. This was a very scary experience for me. We went downtown, he had told me to put on a lot of clothes because it was very cold downtown because of all the high rise buildings. As we were standing at the bus stop waiting for the bus to pick us up, he sneaked inside one of the buildings, when I looked around he was gone and I nearly died. I had no idea what I should do. Lines of buses were coming and I was clueless to which one to get on. I walked to the building immediately behind me. I was shivering both from the cold and being scared, tears were rolled up in my eyes. I sat there on the steps. I was wondering how I missed seeing him get on the bus. I had no one to call or anything. I was sure of one thing I was not leaving that spot, if you get lost downtown Houston you could be lost for days before someone find you. People was staring, they could tell something was wrong. I didn't say anything to anyone, I trusted no one. I had heard horror stories about young ladies especially country ones in big cities. Just when my heart was beating through several layers of clothes, maybe twenty minutes later someone tapped me on my shoulder. I very carefully looked around. It was him, I just stood up and hugged him and started crying. He was testing me and I had passed the test. I made the right decision to stay in that one place and not go wandering all over town. It felt good to be in his arms.

The next several days was quiet, we ate out a few times. We went back downtown around midnight, this time in the car; he wanted to show me the city's real beauty, which to me can only be seen under the moon and starlight. He let the sunroof top back on the car. I sat close in his arms. Everything was breathtaking. It seems the sky was covered in stars and looked as if they were falling down on the buildings.

Before we knew it Sunday rolled around again. This was our last full day and night together. He was returning to work on Monday night.

I got dressed for church and wore a lavender suit and shoes. He said I looked very nice. The church was on the other side of the city in the black neighborhood. It was not the big beautiful church I was expecting. As a matter of fact it was not as nice as the church I had grown up in. It only had a few members most of which were old. Everything was different from what I was use to but I assumed the people and the church would grow on me. It was fun meeting everyone afterward, they were all very nice. This one man in particular, tall, light skinned with clear brown eyes, walked up, hugged me, and gave me a kiss on the cheek, "Welcome to the family," he said. I was caught off guard until he said you must don't know who I am? "No," I said. He was my brother-in-law, and then I saw the resemblance. That night we went back to church for bible school. I had a chance to meet my husband bible teacher. He was in his late nineties and lived to one hundred and four. I loved bible class and I had never heard a man who could teach like him. He had a deep strong compelling voice. His voice commanded your attention and opened your mind to learn. He told me after class he was pleased with the choice my husband had made and that I was going to be a great addition to his ministry. After class we stopped by the drive thru and got some food went home, went to bed, and concluded the honeymoon.

CHAPTER 4

AFTER THE HONEYMOON

WELL, THE HONEYMOON IS OVER and real life as a married couple begins. He asked for the rest of the money to buy groceries. I made out a list and he went across the street and bought the food. I was heartbroken when I knew I wasn't going because I had looked forward to shopping with him. My mama and daddy had always bought grocery together. Daddy would push the cart as mama walked along beside him as they both made choices on what to buy. I was being cheated but I would learn to get use to this over a period of years. My husband loved steak and baked potatoes and broccoli. Later that day I broiled a couple steaks, baked potatoes and broccoli and cheese from the box. I had never baked potatoes or cooked broccoli but everything turned out perfect. He said he had not ever tasted food so good. I took real pleasure in cooking for him. It became routine over the next few weeks and months. Life was the same each day for me. I was in the apartment all day every day. I sat up all night every night scared to even close my eyes. I hated being home alone at night. I had nothing really to watch on television after all I had rules to follow. So, I spent most of my nights reading the bible and taking notes for bible school. On Fridays we went to bible school, on Saturdays it was held at home and back to church and class on Sundays. Every now and then he took me to Pizza Hut on Friday nights. For the most part I was secluded, a poor dog a long ways from home with nowhere to go.

All my mornings was the same, he would arrive home at a quarter to seven I would have already took my bath, have on a sexy night gown and have breakfast on the table. Every other morning it was sausage, eggs, wheat toast, jelly, orange juice, and milk. On the other mornings it was frosted flakes and a glass of orange juice. We'd eat, he'd take a shower and we went to bed. I would always get up before him. I never really had to clean up because the house stayed clean all the time. I would have dinner ready every day by six. This was hard getting use to because in the country dinner was always at twelve noon and in the city it was around six in the evening.

Sometimes after dinner we would play scrabble for hours. Read the newspaper, we bought two so we could compete on the scrambled word finds. I always won. We listened to some of his favorite preachers on the radio and soon it was back to sleep for him so he could get ready for work.

Sometimes he would allow me to ride some places with him. He shopped at K-mart and Target quite often and as we parked I would attempt to open the car door to get out and the reply was always the same, you don't need to get out, I'll be right out and sometimes right out was an hour or two. I would watch all the other couples going in holding hands and before I knew it tears would pour down my face. I've been married almost three months now, living in a big huge city and never once have I been allowed to go in a store. Did you notice I used the word allowed? I was being controlled. I had no say so in my life. By now on Fridays and Sundays he's telling me what I can and cannot wear, how I can and cannot wear my hair, right down to what perfumes I could and could not wear. I was too blind by my respect for him to see my life was being manipulated and controlled and God had nothing to do with it.

Yes, you heard me right God had nothing to do with this. God is all about love and compassion and only commands us to love and obey our husbands in the Lord. This was not about God this was about you better do what I say, when I say, and the or else came within a matter of weeks.

There are some of you right now who see yourselves in this situation. It is one thing to say I don't like your hair like that or I don't like your outfit, but its control and abuse to say take it off and put on something else and redo your hair or stay here. These are signs to what will someday become a very abusive person. You should be allowed to wear what you want within moderation and to do your hair as you wish within moderation.

If he likes a certain outfit or hairstyle then by all means wear it sometimes just for him. You want to make him happy.

Don't ever give in to control and manipulation you will learn to regret it. You have to make a stand for yourself, or always be kicked down.

It is not about who is in control it's about the both of you being happy. I should not have sat in the heat and the cold in the car while he enjoyed shopping in the stores. I should not have been pushed around by what to wear and not wear. From day one of knowing him I gave him permission to mistreat me. I thought I was being a good wife to suffer inside and never say anything about what I was feeling. I was disgusted and no one knew it but me and God. I talked to mama every day and never told her how unhappy I was about some things. I was bored, lonely, and setting myself up for years of depression. My faith, my hope, my trust in God kept me going.

I think my parents doctrine you made your bed hard lay in it merely ruined me. My bed was uncomfortable but I stayed in it. No one could ever know that two such holy people were not happy together.

I was trying so hard to be happy with him. Some nights I would bathe him, I gave him pedicures, I washed his hair, I shined his shoes every Saturday night, I would lie so close to him until my side of the bed was never disturbed.

I was trying everything within my power to make him show me love. It was not happening. I love him but I was not feeling what I was putting in. Sex with him was good or at least, I thought it was. I had not and still have not been with any other person. I was satisfied with his skills. No place was off limits to him. The bathroom, living room, kitchen, dining room, closet, you get the picture. From this point we were like newlyweds. I guess something was better than nothing at all.

We had our love for God in common. We had sex and almost nothing else. Our conversation was almost always about the word of God. We were respectfully gaining knowledge of God's word but we were not learning anything about one another.

We knew nothing about one another. We didn't even know one another likes and dislikes and how would we ever if we didn't start really talking to one another.

CHAPTER 5

MARRIED LIFE BEGINS

THE HONEYMOON IS OVER AND real life begins. Cooking and cleaning has been a part of my life as long as I can remember. Things are continuing to spin in different directions. I'm still sitting in parking lots not allowed to go in stores.

He noticed I had been holding my bible too close to my face so he took me to an eye specialist. The news was nothing I expected. I was twenty-two years old and I hear, "Mrs. Shirley, you are losing your eyesight, you will probably be blind in a matter of months," the doctor said.

Needless to say, I froze in my tracks. I could not stop crying. Strangers were trying to comfort me but nothing worked.

I went home and called my mama, it tore her apart. She could not believe it.

Before I knew it, it was time for Friday night bible class. As Elder Mingo stood and expounded on the lesson, "The Works of the Holy Spirit," I knew I needed the Holy Spirit to work on me. After the review I stood and asked Elder if I could say something. Through a heart full of tears I explained what the doctor said about my eyes. The cornea was not flat anymore; it was shaped like a cone and was completely blind in the back of my eye. This was the left eye but the disease of the left eye was overworking the right eye and therefore was deteriorating both eyes.

"Come to me daughter," Elder said. He called my husband, "my boy," and me, daughter. He had ten children of his own but was closer to my husband than he was to his own children. They were not Christians so he did not have a spiritual bond with them.

My husband and I walked to the front of the old church. He asked the sisters to sing a praise song. He asked the pastor and my husband to join him. He took the anointed oil and poured it over the top of my head. Then as I closed my eyes he anointed them. I immediately knew God had done something supernatural. He told us to go the next day and find another eye doctor, your sight will not be perfect, but God said you are not going blind. I felt so much better, a weight lifted from me. I went home and called my mama after he left for work. She informed me that everyone there was praying for me. She also told me that the preacher I use to sing and pray with wanted me to call him. After hanging up with her I immediately called him. Just hearing his voice lifted me. I was so glad to talk to him. He told me to go in the restroom and wash out my eyes in the name of the Father, Son, and the Holy Spirit. I did just as he said and felt even better.

The next day we went down the street from our home to see a doctor by the name of Dr. Black.

He assured me that I wasn't losing my sight but that my left eye cornea was deformed an in serious need of repair. He was only an optometrist so there was not anything he could do for me. He could not write a prescription for glasses because he was not use to the disease I had. Therefore, he referred me to an ophthalmologist.

We went to see him the next week. He was amazed at how my cornea looked. He told me I needed a cornea transplant immediately.

Here I was, a country girl a long ways from home, whom had never been to an eye doctor hearing all this. He explained to me what a transplant was. I would be receiving a cornea from a deceased person, a donor. My husband had a problem with this he refused to let me have the surgery. I did not understand this, it was my eye, and it should have been my decision. Almost five years later I received my first transplant, now I have had two on the left eye and one on the right.

In all reality I know now if I could do things differently I would have had the surgery immediately. I know he was afraid I probably would lose my eyesight completely. The doctor explained that it was a possibility I could lose my sight. However to me it was a part of prayers answered a part of my healing. He was able to write me a prescription; my glasses were as thick as a coke bottle and literally made me nauseated while getting use to them. After weeks I began to get use to them and it fascinated me to know how much of the world I was missing out on. I was so used to seeing with one eye, I was not aware of it. I could see faces now, colors, I didn't look good but I felt very good.

Well, the old Shirley is a part of the past and a new Shirley is born. A sad, broken unhappy person is taking me over. I'm bored, lonely, and crying more than I ever have. I didn't know what was wrong with me. Life was not about me anymore, nothing mattered about Shirley, it was about him. Everything I did now was about pleasing him. I thought so sure that this was what God expected of me. I buried myself and became the idea and thought of what a perfect wife was.

I never wanted to make him mad or see him unhappy. I literally kissed his feet and his butt to make him happy, make him love me. In all you do and as much of yourself as you give you will not ever make a person love you.

My husband and going to church was my life. I had nothing else. No friends, I had nothing else.

I had one little thing in my life other than the above mentioned. A good church friend of mine had given me a little stuffed puppy as a wedding gift, he sat on my bed each day. She told me when I was feeling lonely or homesick to pick it up and think of her, my family, and church family. Sometimes I would hold it all night when he was at work. Sometimes he would catch me during the day picking it up placing it next to my heart. He said I want you to get rid of that, you are treating it like an idol. So his suggestion was to throw it away. I tried to make a stand for myself. I asked him did he have things from other girls or friends that he should be getting rid of. He went to his brother's house and brought back a box of pictures of girls from his past. I think this was more about hurting me than getting rid of old pictures. There was a picture of him kissing a white girl, he said he was engaged to her but things didn't work out.

We tore all the pictures up and he went to the trash dumpster with the box with my poor Pookie inside. I went in the restroom and cried not only had I thrown away a gift but I felt like I threw away my friend Darlene who bought it. This was all about control, making me do as he commanded.

Well, weeks went by and I got a phone call from back home. My sister wanted to spend the summer with me. She wanted to find a job before going back to college. Surprisingly, he said it was okay. I was so happy, this meant I would have company, someone to talk to.

I had to go over all the rules with her, no smoking, no wearing pants in the apartment, and others I don't remember.

She came and I truly enjoyed her short stay. He did not want her to work, or meet any people or anything and fortunately she's one of those ladies who do not let anyone push her around.

Things happened why she was visiting. Secrets! Secrets! Secrets! This would be the beginning of what would be years of mental and physical abuse.

We had planned this big dinner for his three brothers and their children. We were all dressed and ready to go to the store. This time I had to go because he did not want my sister to know he didn't let me go in the stores with him.

We went in to buy all the food we needed, it came down to making a decision about what dessert to choose. I personally could forever do without sweets but I thought I was looking out for the best interest of others. My sister chose a lemon pie and so did he. I asked him if it would be okay to get a chocolate pie, he said no. I tried explaining that most children love chocolate and not lemon. Lo said we'll put my pie back and get chocolate but I would not do that because she was a special guest also. I said it was okay so we paid for the food, less one chocolate pie and went home. He went straight home. We started putting the grocery away. He said, "You know something I changed my mind. I'm going back and get the chocolate pie," he said. There I stood smiling and happy. "Come go with me Shirley, your sister can put the food away," he said. She agreed.

I sat in the car while he went in and got the pie. "Is this the one you wanted so badly?" he asked. It was the exact one. We drove away but in a different direction than our apartment. We drove down the back street pass the grocery store. He stopped the car, I asked what was wrong and where were we going.

"You wanted that pie awfully bad didn't you," he said. Something was wrong, something was different. His beautiful, sexy, brown eyes were fiery and fierce looking. He was angry! Real angry!

I kept asking what was wrong. "You embarrassed me! You don't embarrass me! What I say is what goes!" I kept explaining how sorry I was and that I would never do it again. I really didn't know what I had done but I was sure of one thing I would never do it again.

I was so scared I was trembling. It started, the abuse started. He took a hair rake, that's a comb made of metal, used for combing afros. He hit me in the top of my head with the sharp ends of the prongs. When I tried to grab the comb he started hitting my hands and arms. Blood was coming from the little holes the comb was leaving. He snatched my head back by my hair and repeatedly hit me. Blood was coming down in my face. I was in shock, he's a preacher he could not possibly be doing this. He kept calling me fat and ugly over and over. I don't remember if I cried. Three months into my marriage and this was happening. I tried to get out the car, I was on my knees. He had control of the locks on his side so he locked the door so. I couldn't get out. He started hitting me on the back of my legs with the comb. By now I was hurting so bad, I was tired. He said clean up yourself and comb you hair so we can leave. I took Kleenexes from the box and cleaned my face the best I could, combed my hair and we went back to the apartment. I went straight to the restroom and washed away the blood so that Lo would not see it. I didn't know how to act but acting is just what I did. I deserve a Grammy for all the acting I have done over a period of years.

My sister and I got all the food prepared for the next day meal. Okay I did well. I concealed a secret; I protected him from a shame and embarrassment.

We went to bed and a series of what would forever take place, he would get turned on after beating me and I would make up to him by having sex with him. No, you did not read this line wrong and no, I did not write it wrong. This is exactly what I did, he beat me and I begged forgiveness and made up to him.

The next morning came and I was so sore until I could barely move. Every part of me was hurting. I took a bath and got dressed.

My head was so sore until I couldn't comb my hair; I just kind of pulled it back and didn't worry about it. Soon all our guest arrived and dinner was served. I was right, none of the children liked the lemon pie and neither did his oldest brother. The chocolate went first. All his nieces and nephews fell in love with my sister, so did one of his brothers. He made sure nothing came of this although his brother tried very hard. I'm glad it didn't work out because a year later God dropped her husband right from the sky.

A few weeks went by and he did not hit me again. I was sure it was a one-time thing that would never happen again. I dare to say if a man hit you once he will hit you again!!! My sister, is back at home, back in school, and I'm all alone again most of the time.

We've started talking about having a baby. I was so ready for a little girl. We found a clinic called Norwell Center which would help me lose the weight I needed to lose in order to get pregnant.

I was so restricted until I couldn't even eat a peppermint. I hated this diet with a passion but the doctor assured me I would get pregnant this way.

A baby was just what I needed. I needed someone to fill the void, the loneliness, the emptiness that was hidden deep within my heart. One morning around six I went in the kitchen to fix my diet drink like I had done every morning for months. The awful smell of it and the taste was dreadful, this morning it was especially hard to even put it in my mouth. I ran to the restroom and literally threw up my guts. I was so sick until I almost passed out. I called him at work and told him what was going on. He joked and said I bet you anything you're pregnant. I doubted that because I still had fifteen or twenty pounds to lose.

Later that morning he took me to an OBGYN doctor and sure enough he was right. I was so happy I did not know how to act. He seemed as happy as me. I was six weeks pregnant. I rushed home and called mama. I don't think I'd ever heard her so excited. I just could not believe I was going to have a baby. Me the girl who had played with dolls until I was thirteen or fourteen. Now, I would have my very own baby. A baby girl is what I wanted more than anything in the world. We went out to eat to celebrate. I could actually eat anything I wanted and not have to be concerned about gaining any weight. It took weeks to get use to eating again. We made our announcement to the church over the weekend and the next week I took my first trip to the mall. We went maternity shopping. He bought me a lot of beautiful dresses. Mama had a lot of dresses made for me as well. I loved being pregnant. It was not anything about it I didn't like. I didn't have a lot of morning sickness but I did have night sickness.

Elder had taught us how to have children for God so I did everything I'd been taught. Even before conceiving the baby I'd pray all through the day that God would give me a blessed anointed baby. I sung gospel songs all through the day, I listened to gospel music, and I read the bible aloud to my baby all the time every day. The bible declares that we are shaped in sin, so I wanted to do all I could to instill a spiritual mind in my baby as well.

Well, an incident happened that unfortunately would cause my second beating which would prove to be far worse than the first. A man called to speak to my husband one night around nine or ten. He asked me who was I and mistakenly, unfortunately I told the truth, I said I'm his wife. He demanded that I hang the phone up immediately, so I did. As soon as I put the receiver down he grabbed me and gave me one blow to the head one after the other. I was bent over trying my best to protect my baby. He threw me to the floor, I turned over and lay on my stomach, and he pulled off his belt and whipped me like an angry father might whip his child. He went on and on. I thought he would never stop. I tried my best to scream but he held my mouth so tight until I could barely breathe. When I finally could get some air I begged him to stop but he would not. After about thirty minutes the phone rang, it was the man again he had pulled the cot out because he said I will not be sleeping with you tonight. He told his friend to hold on. I was in the bathroom trying to compose myself. I was hurting so badly but mainly my head; I had been hit in my head so much until I could taste blood in my mouth.

"You are going to come in here and give me some first aid, and you going to do it now, Get in here!," he commanded. I learned that night that first aid meant oral sex. There he lay stretched out on his back on the cot, talking to his friend while I was there on my knees giving him first aid. Being the idiot I was when he was done I got a pillow and lay on the floor beside the cot. I was determined I would not spend a night not sleeping with him. We were taught that you should not be apart in the bed unless one of you was fasting. The next morning we got up for church, I wore long sleeves to make sure all the whelps and scratches were covered. I wanted to protect him; I did not want anyone to think badly of him because he was a preacher.

Our pastor had a bad heart condition which he died of a few years later so my husband preached every Sunday. This Sunday he told the church he had a special treat for them. He called me up to sing a solo, it was my first time. It seemed that there was not a dry eye in the church including mine.

I find that when I sing my hurt comes out through my voice. I can almost never sing without crying.

Now, strangely enough I did not look at him as a hypocrite or a phony person. I truly believe he loved God with all his heart both then and now. However, he had a serious problem, one that could prove to be fatal.

I learned to smile through my tribulations, my abuse. I learned to have joy in spite of. I thought on things that made me happy. Every day I looked forward to the day I would hold my precious baby in my arms.

The beatings were now coming more often. It seemed anything was an excuse to be hit. Another thing that is becoming more apparent is the fact of how ashamed of me he is. I've learned now the reasons I've only been in a store with him once or twice. He told me I was fat and ugly and he hated to be seen with me.

There was a preacher who came to one of the big churches in Houston to do a revival. I loved his preaching. My husband made plans to go and hear him preach. I wanted so much to go but he said no almost every night, on the last night he told me I could go but I could not sit with him. He said a lot of his friends and co-workers were going to be there and he did not want them to know what he was married to. I enjoyed myself so much and it didn't matter that he sat with his friends and not me. All that mattered was that I was there and the guest preacher was there. As I was leaving out to go to the car which was parked away from the other cars he came to me to remind me not to come near him.

Unfortunately, some of his nosy lady friends were watching and saw him talking to me. They all came rushing over to meet me. They were asking is this your wife, she's so cute, she have beautiful hair, when is the baby due? The questions went on and on. I thought I was looking decent, I had on a royal blue maternity with pink and white pinstripes, matching shoes and hat but apparently it wasn't good enough for him.

When we got in the car and drove down the street he struck me in my head and said, I asked you not to embarrass me. I told you to leave straight out and stay away from me. I tried to explain that he was the one who came to me but he struck me again. He said when I get you home you are going to wish you had never asked to come with me. When we arrived home he rushed in. I was hoping everything was over but this night would teach me that if he said something he meant it. An event took place that would happen over and over for years to come. He closed the door and stood on the side so when I opened the door he would be behind

THE SECRET LIFE OF A PREACHER'S WIFE

it and when I closed the door I looked right in his face and he immediately jumped me. This would happen many times to come and would scare me just as bad each time.

He went in the room after hitting me in the head several times and got his exercising jump rope, it had a wooden handle attached to the ends of the rope. I wondered what was he going to do with it, but I didn't wonder long. He started to whip me with it striking me over and over again with the wooden handles. This would also be the night he would start pulling my hair, he pulled patches out from the roots, yelling, you think your hair is so much but it doesn't mean anything to me. My hair is not even half as long as it was then and I always believe it will not grow back because it was snatched out. When things were over I crawled around the house picking up my hair, put it in a Ziploc bag and hid it under one of the kitchen drawers. Each time my hair would get pulled out I'd hide it in the bag. I don't know if I was keeping it as evidence of the abuse or just could not bear throwing it away. He was right a woman's hair was her glory and I loved my hair passionately. I feel so different about my hair now. It's like he ripped the love for my hair out of me as well. It's much shorter now and although I'm just forty-five it's almost salt and pepper. However, I love the gray hair and look forward to the day it's all gray.

Well, the beatings are more often now and seem to get more severe each time. I hide the ropes as fast as he buys them so now he uses his belts instead. When I was a little girl if my mom would whip me she would always put Vaseline on my scars. I never thought I would be doing the same thing to myself as a grown woman. Yet, after being whipped like an unloved child I'd get the medicated Vaseline and put it on my scars. He would walk around in the apartment looking for the belts like a mad man. I recall being so nervous thinking he would find them. I had one hid in the vegetable tray of the refrigerator, one in the bottom of the china cabinet, and one behind the china cabinet. He never wanted to use his church belt. I guess he considered it sacred. However if things got bad enough he would use it time to time. He never once found my hiding spots. I had told myself many times if he couldn't find the belts he wouldn't hit me. I was so wrong nothing or no one could ever stop him.

It was becoming so obvious to me he didn't love me and he was very ashamed of me. I wasn't his type he would tell me. I wasn't tall enough, I wasn't skinny and I wasn't light skinned enough. I think this made it much easier for him to hit me. If I had been beautiful and sexy he wouldn't have hit me. This is a fantasy. I've learned he didn't hit me because of me he hit because of his own insecurities and problems of his own. Most of which dealt with his family history.

However, when he would think of how I looked, my less than perfect skin, my obesity, and my out of shape figure it truly made it easier for him to beat me. My life, my world, had become protecting my baby, I would have rather been hit in the head than any other place than to risk losing my baby.

Some days he was actually sweet and nice I just never knew how long it would last. He could be happy one minute and mad as hell the next. I was always on my p's and q's in our conversation, hoping I always said the right thing. If I said I never had any happy times with him I would not be telling the truth. Some days were memorable and some weren't. Coming home for Christmas holidays was a lot of fun. I was barely showing but yet I couldn't wait for mama to see my stomach. Both she and my Aunt could not stop laughing. I had been one of the shyest young girls growing up. When I was thirteen I wore a pink sweater the entire summer to hide my newly developed breast. This time I couldn't hide the little package inside my stomach.

The holidays were great. He spent most of his time with his family and I spent mine with my family. He ate Christmas dinner at both houses. I was hundreds of miles from Texas and so were all of my problems. For the next week I was the happiest person in the world. I was with my family and it felt great. Mama cooked everything she thought I wanted for dinner every day. It felt so good to be back in my bed again. My aunt slept with me every night so I wouldn't be cold. Winter nights could be pretty cold in our country home. Before I knew it the week was over and we were back at home. Both his mom and mine had given us pies, cakes, and all the works to bring home with us. The next few months was magical, no arguing, no fighting.

When he was able to be home at night it was a very special time. He would be as excited as me to feel the baby kicking in his back. He would joke he had a little quarterback growing inside of me. It seemed I was getting bigger every day and I absolutely loved it.

I still wasn't going to a lot of stores with him but I was getting more and more use to it. We did go out to eat sometimes on the weekend.

I had accepted my life for what it was and decided to make the best of it.

I am in my sixth month now and stomach is getting bigger and bigger. It seems when things are pretty normal in your life the devil has his way of messing things up.

It was a Saturday night about nine o'clock p.m. We had our regular Saturday evening bible class. He had taken Elder home and came back to the apartment. We played scrabble and was about to go to bed when someone knocked on the door. He looked out the window and told me to answer the door and say he wasn't home. When I opened the door a young lady was standing there.

"Who are you?" she said. I asked her the same question. I am a friend of his. I met him at the laundry mat and I was just stopping by to check on him. "Tell her you are my wife", he said. So I did.

Tell her not to ever come back here again, so I did. She explained that she did not mean any harm. She looked as if she had been working at a fast food restaurant, she had flour all over her clothes and a head full of rollers. It was hard to tell how she looked, but she looked okay. When she left he explained how he met her and why she probably stopped by. He said I treated her cold and was out of my place to do so. He said I had no right to mistreat one of his friends. I tried to explain that I had only said what he wanted me to. Before I knew it I was slapped on the floor. I could not believe he was hitting me for something he told me to do. I asked him if the girl did not mean anything to him why was he beating me about her. This night things progressed worse than ever. I crumpled over on the floor trying to protect my stomach. He was careful not to hit me in the stomach giving me one blow after another in my head. I remember my head hurting so bad until I was pleading and begging with him to stop. He grabbed me around the throat demanding that I be quiet before the neighbors heard me. His grasp got tighter and tighter until I could no longer breathe. I was patting my hands against the floor trying to convey that I could not breathe, words was trying hard to come out, "Please, please I can't breathe!" Just before death came it seems he turned me a loose. I was so afraid, more afraid than I've ever been in my life; I just knew he was going to kill me. In a matter of minutes he was undressing me to make love. This was his sick way of making up to me. I had to lie there and pretend that all was well always forgiving him no matter what he had done. This girl was never mentioned again, I never even knew her name. All I knew was if I never saw her again it would not matter to me.

It seems the beating came more regular now and the reasons could have been most anything. I was getting my eyeglasses fixed on a weekly basis from being broken while being beat in the head. Soon I would learn to quickly pull them off and put them away.

A few weeks passed by and a similar situation took place. Another young lady came by, he instructed me over the same routine. I tried to be very careful to say exactly what he told me. She said her mother was sick and needed prayer. This young lady had a very nasty attitude; she was very, very rude. My husband had to come to the door to calm her down. He instructed me to go in the bedroom he'd handle it. I went in the bedroom; soon I heard the door slam. Naturally, I assumed she left but instead he went outside with her. I finally built up my nerves to see if he had left with her. He was leaning over in her car talking to her. This had been about thirty minutes. He said go back inside its okay I'll be in in a minute. I asked her to leave and not to come back again. I later learned that he had been involved with her as more than a friend and that night she really came by for money. I don't think he gave her any. I went inside knowing I had made a grave mistake. He beat me senseless that night. He went crazy! His whole demeanor changed. I feared for my life more than ever. He got me between the bed and the wall and hit me over and over again both with his fist and the belt. He choked me until my eyes closed; somehow I managed to put one of my hands under the quilt on the window. I was praying someone would come and rescue me. He saw me take my hand out and stomped it. Every time I tried to scream he would choke me harder.

You know, I cannot explain the fear I would feel when he would choke me. Scared is not the right word, it was beyond any explanation. My heart would beat out my body and as long as I remained sane my thought would be focused on God, begging him to please spare my life. Just when I would think everything was over he'd turn me a loose. My throat would hurt for days. Lying there patting my hands on the floor and kicking my legs up and down to get his attention was horrible. I felt so useless, so low, so down, I just could not believe I was going through this. I later learned that there is one spot in your throat if touched with pressure it would kill you on the spot. This frightened me even more, God truly kept me. The following Sunday I went to church and acted as if nothing had happened. I wasn't able to sing because my voice was gone.

Although I'd been to hell and back the night before I didn't let it keep me down. I went to church smiling every Sunday, fixed up and trying to look my best.

I have often wondered what would click in him, what would make him so angry. How could a preacher beat the wife he had asked God for? I hated what he was doing to me physically and mentally. However, spiritually this was giving me a walk and a close relationship with God that I had never experienced. I had to depend on God. I had to trust him like never before. For the first time I truly knew that my life was in God's control. God was so good to me. When I would go for my checkups my scars would be healed and my doctor acted as if he didn't suspect anything. God protected my baby and no harm came to her.

Sometimes after a beating he would go out and get things I liked such as candy or fish. He began very successfully to convince me he was sorry for the pain he inflicted on me. We never talked about it, sometimes I truly wanted to but I knew if I would have chances or it would have started again.

I was beginning to feel ashamed for what I was going through. I felt like everything was my fault. I felt like if I had been skinny or beautiful he would not do this to me. I felt in a sense I must deserve what I was going through. I didn't think God wanted me to be abused but I felt like he did not want me to bring a shame or disgrace on my husband. I felt it was my duty to protect him. I did not talk to him about it because I did not want him to feel ashamed. I remember so many times making up to him for making him hit me. I blamed myself, if I had not done this or said that he would not have beaten me. It took me twenty years to learn that this was not my fault. This was a sickness and a madness that was dwelling deep within him. Something caused this, something deeper than me. Talk about the abuse if you are going through it, tell someone, talk to your pastor, a neighbor, a friend, a policeman, please talk to someone. It is never the right thing to do to hold this in to keep a secret. I know there are other preacher wives being abused. We see the glamour of the pastor and the first lady, we hear him preach the word, sing the Zion songs, wear the best suits, we see her dressed in the best attire, with matching hats and shoes and we'd never guess the hell she's living through.

Most preachers never express their disappointments, anger, heartbreaks to the church members but the wives know it all. The preachers have a holier than thou attitude with the people but the wives see the real man the one you don't see.

My abuse continued throughout my pregnancy, it was a secret between me, my husband, and God.

CHAPTER 6

GOING HOME TO HAVE THE BABY

I WAS ENTERING MY EIGHTH month of pregnancy and this meant a trip back home to Mississippi. I was excited, relieved, and felt down right free. Close to my ninth month I came home to have the baby. We drove home in a new Lincoln we had purchased. We looked as if though life was well and we were living the best of life. We were living big, but in reality I felt like a small potato. I was more than happy to be home. Things were different this time. I was treated so special but the months of abuse had taken its course. I was sad and broken and all the attention in Mississippi couldn't change it. I could not fool my mom she did not know I was abused but she knew I acted different and strange. She'd catch me sometimes staring in the middle of nowhere. I tried to explain to her that I missed my husband but I'm sure she knew it was something more. Each time you are hit or mentally abused it seems to take an inch of your life away. Writing this book has brought back hurt and pain that had been hidden inside of me for years.

The week passed by and before I knew it the baby was on her way. My husband had made his arrival and we went to the hospital early

Friday morning, I had a very long painful delivery. My husband showed his mean, hateful side and did not want my family to come in while I was in labor. After many hours of pain and agony our baby girl made her arrival. This was one of the happiest days of my life. We had a beautiful baby girl. I won't talk a lot about my children in this book. I want to protect their rights and privacy and also leave them room to write their own story someday. I left back for Houston a week later. My nine year old niece went to help me out. Her stay was very short. One night when the baby was about a month old, I needed to walk to the store to get something for dinner. The store was about a three or four minute walk. The baby was sleeping and I both bottle fed and breast fed her. I told my husband if she wake up before I came back to give her a bottle and I would breastfeed her in the next feeding. This was not good enough for him, he insisted that I wake her up, breast feed her, and then leave. She was on a schedule and it wasn't time to feed her.

He woke her up, brought her in the room and said, now she's awake, feed her. Something inside of me just exploded. These were my breast, my baby that I suffered and brought in this world and he was forcing me to do something. It was all about control. Do what I say, when I say do it! I guess I was just tired and embarrassed. My nine year old niece was standing there waiting to see what was going to happen. I walked back in the bedroom, put the baby in the bed and waited for him to make his first move. He pushed me over and over again, not hitting me just pushing me around. Jerking my hair and talking loud. Finally, I heard my niece crying. I pleaded with him to stop insisting he was scaring her out her mind. I knew she had seen others do this before but I could not do this to her. I begged him to calm down but it seemed all my pleading was in vain. He started choking me. Somehow I managed to get my hands on a little red metal bowl he had sitting on the dresser full of change. I threw it against the wall hoping that the noise would distract him. However, it only scared my niece worse and as a result of everything that took place she called her mama. She decided to leave immediately and come and get her. My husband called them and said when you get her make plans to take your sister with you. He packed all my clothes and the baby clothes. I packed all my niece things while crying the entire time. I hated so much to see her go, but I knew in my heart I loved my husband and I was not leaving him.

The next morning came and somewhere between nine and ten they knocked on the door. It was my mom, my sister, and one of my brothers. My husband put all the stuff outside as he greeted my family as if nothing had happened. His brother was waiting outside in his car unknowingly to my family. I told them he was there and went inside and sat down. One thing I was sure of, my husband and I had made our bed hard and we had to lay in it. My parents had taught us this all our lives and I wasn't going to let anything change now. I explained to them that I was not leaving and begged them to put my things back in the house. Some part of me wanted to leave and some part wanted my marriage to work so badly. I was determined that Satan would not win. My husband went got my things out of the car. My mama held on to my baby girl as if to say, I will not allow you to keep her here. She got in the car and drove away with my baby. I was running after the car crying and begging them to stop so I could get my baby. Eventually they drove back around and gave the baby to my husband. He tried to assure me that things would be different and he was glad I stayed. He told me to get dressed, took me out to lunch and it seemed all was well. It seemed we would never argue again or at least that's what I told myself. I knew my husband had problems but surely through prayer I could change him. Later that day, I went through the task of hanging my clothes and putting away the baby things. Well, a few weeks passed by and everything was peaches and cream, however this did not last.

He became angry about something, went into a rage and beat me silly. He pulled down all my clothes, threw them to the floor, knocked all my shoes off the shelves and shoved me in the closet.

I had a big walk in closet and it became routine for me to lock myself in it to get away from the abuse. It became routine for him to pull down my hundreds of clothes each time he'd hit me. It was easy now for him to hit me and reasons didn't matter, sometimes I feel he would hit me just because I was breathing. My baby would soon be turning a year old and already she'd probably heard me being hit a hundred times. He would put her away in the bedroom as if he was ashamed to let her see him hit me.

My only comfort after being beat was to take her in my arms and sing to her. She loved music and she loved my singing. Sometimes my tears would wet her little clothes as they dropped from my eyes on to her.

She was a beautiful perfect little girl. How could someone so beautiful come from such messed up parents. I would pray and beg God to please not allow any of what she was hearing to affect her. Today she's a beautiful young lady whom loves God with all her heart. She's twenty-two now and as you will see the abuse continued her entire life. Abuse is a nasty, awful, dangerous situation to live in. Not every person live to tell about being abused and if you do you should tell others about it.

The first year of my baby life was one of the most dreadful times of my life. I thought life had been tough growing up on a farm, being reared by a daddy who would cuss me sometimes as if though I was not his child. I would have given anything to get those days back. Anything was better than this.

I can't express the hurt, the disappointment, the shame that I was feeling. I had become a broken hearted, let down, disgusted, sick person. By now I looked different, I acted different, and acted is what I did. I held everything inside of me. I truly was a preacher's wife with a secret life and the secrets were tearing me apart day by day. I had no one that I trusted to tell what I was going through. My husband had lost his good paying job. The factory he worked for was closing down and he had been laid-off for months. His unemployment was running out and life as we knew it was about to become worse. There is one thing I must say about him, he was a hard worker and he did all he could for me and my baby not to suffer for food and shelter. He took every job he was offered but would be laid-off it seems in no time at all. I sometimes think this pressure contributed even more to his constant abuse. A man has a lot of pride and his pride was being tested.

I woke up one morning very sick. I thought it was a result of my constant dieting to keep my weight off. After going to the doctor I learned I was pregnant with my second child. I was extremely happy. Although times were difficult I knew God was going to take care of me. This time things would be different, I could no longer afford a private doctor so I had to go to the welfare clinic instead. I hated this but I endured it. We made plans to move to a bigger apartment in the same complex. The manager was patient with us. We were getting further and further behind on the rent. I was good at knitting so I started making products from yarn and my husband would sale them to the ladies on his job. This was allowing us to bring in extra money every week but it was deteriorating my eyes more and more.

He was laid-off that job so both his income stopped and mine. He had not been on the job long enough to get unemployment so for the first time we had no income at all.

I was not used to hard times. I had grown up in a home where we never had to want for food, was never ever not worried one time that we would not have a place to live.

I was scared sick but I tried to keep a positive attitude. Somehow we managed to keep food on the table. I never told my parents about our financial problems. His brothers were a big help to us financially.

In all this you would think we would be so busy praying until we would not have time for anything else. I continued singing and praying and reading the bible to my little girl and the little boy I was carrying inside of me. I know that God placed a special anointing on my children because of this.

We were well into our second year of marriage close to our third year. Our baby boy was born one month before our third year anniversary. I had just begged God for a little boy preacher and he gave him to me. My little girl was two years old and she was already singing solo's in church.

My mom and my Aunt had made plans to leave the day after my baby boy was born. I was the happiest person in the world. I had my son on a Friday evening and was home on a Saturday evening. A couple hours before they were to leave Mississippi my husband changed his mine. He said you don't need any help; I'll be here to help you. Call them and tell them not to come.

I begged him, I cried, I pleaded with him to please let them come. I wanted to see them so bad and was so embarrassed to tell them they couldn't come. He told me he was going to K-Mart to get films to take pictures of the baby. He said when he get back it would be good if I had already called and stopped them.

When he arrived back he asked me did I call them. "No," I replied. He assured me if they came he wasn't going to the bus station to pick them up. He rushed and called them, they were just walking out the door. He said he had thought about it and he just preferred to take care of me himself. It was around nine p.m. both the children were asleep. I sat crumpled in the chair, sore, tired and crying my eyes out. I had had a difficult labor, was very anemic and felt awful all over. He hung the phone up and started laughing in my face asking me did I need any help getting to the bed, I just cried even more as he replied you want something to cry for, he hit me across the head, I told you to call them and you didn't. You don't disobey me, he kept saying. He dragged me out the chair; I was so sore and weak until I didn't have any strength to fight back. He was pulling me up and down the floor, kicking and hitting me repeatedly.

"I just had a baby you are going to kill me." I begged him to stop, I could feel the blood pouring down my legs but nothing would stop him.

He just kept hitting me and kicking me. When he finally stopped I crawled to the restroom where I tried to clean myself up. I went in my bedroom and crawled in the bed. He asked me was I still bleeding real badly. I was scared to say yes, I just replied, I'm okay. He told me I didn't look right, you just go to sleep and I'll take care of the baby tonight. He was very good at helping with our first baby so I trusted him to take care of our little boy. I lay there hurting so bad, my head hurt from being hit in it, my stomach was cramping and my legs hurt from being kicked on. As I was falling asleep I could feel the warm blood running down my legs, I knew I should have been in the emergency room but I did not have the nerves to say so. I went into such a deep sleep until I didn't even hear the baby cry through the night. The next morning when I finally woke up I was full of blood. He said some of the church members coming over so you need to get yourself fixed up. I did not want to be bothered; I just wanted to be left alone. I was still hurting, still bleeding heavily and did not feel like pretending to be the HAPPY NEW MOTHER. I just wanted to crawl in the nearest corner and die. My mother called to check on me. I could barely talk to her without crying. She thought I was just hoarse and sounding rough because I'd just had the baby. Life had thrown me a blow and I just did not like it at all. I was glad when the people came and left. I immediately went to bed. The next day I was back at the hospital hemorrhaging. They sent me back home and told me to stay off my feet. He acted as if he felt bad for what he had done but this time was different for me. He had torn something in me that made me know my life would not ever be the same.

It hurts so bad to give birth to a baby. I had midwives so I had a natural delivery, no drugs at all. Having a baby messed with my brains it would take weeks for me to feel like myself, but he had made things even worse for me. The blows to my head left me disoriented for days. I felt empty. It seemed a part of my heart was missing. My only joy was my two babies. I poured my life into my children. This week changed my life, somehow I lost Shirley, she no longer existed, and everything was about my husband and my children. I never thought about what I wanted to eat, it was about what my husband wanted. I promise you in some sense I literally buried myself and rebirthed a new life for them.

Within a few weeks we moved in the other apartment. I so wanted to leave all the abuse all our problems in the old place. I convinced myself that we were starting over. I begged him to promise he would never hit me again. He couldn't even lie, nothing had changed, and he just had an extra room to beat me in. Before long I was being beat there.

We received our first eviction notice. I didn't even know what this meant he just told me to start packing because we were going to move. We were under some very critical times and he really began to show an even worse side. Things got so out of hand one night until he got the phone and called my daddy to come and get me. My daddy, my brothers and one of my sisters drove almost five hundred miles to pick me up. I'm sure tempers were boiling in that truck; by the time they made it to the apartment. About seven a.m. they knocked on the door. He would not even unlock the door for them. I peeked through the peep hole to let them know I was alright. They exchanged a few words and left. They left again without me. A few days later the manager turned our lights off.

We were too far behind on our rent so we just moved across town to another apartment.

CHAPTER 7

A SHORT VACATION

THIS IS THE THIRD YEAR of our marriage. We are already in our third year of marriage and life is not getting any better mentally or physically.

Spiritually my life was in better check than ever. I have now learned to totally depend on God. My prayer life is better than ever I have so much now to pray about. As a matter of fact God and my two babies have become my reason for living. I sometimes think if I did not have my two children and my hope and faith in God I would have taken my life. It was hard to get out of bed most mornings. I had to drag myself to the tub and in the kitchen to fix breakfast for my husband and my baby girl.

More and more bill collectors are calling with threats and demands. Sometimes I would just turn the answering machine on to not be bothered. It's amazing that the lady from the phone company, Mrs. Taylor, knew me on a first name basis because I called her so much getting extensions on our phone bill. One day she and I got in a long conversation about a company that had just hired her son. It was a meat packing company. One of her friends who was a manager had hired him. I asked her would she put in a good word for my husband. A few days later he had the job. Sometimes she would just call to check on me. She was a very devout Christian who loved helping people.

My husband again had the grave yard shift. I didn't like this but we were both happy he was back at work. He had to wear layers of clothes because the building was so cold.

I missed having him home at night, in spite of his abuse sometimes I still felt safer with him around.

My brother in law called and asked did I want to go home to Mississippi. I was so happy. My husband didn't go but me and my two children did. I was so glad to be home. The first day we arrived, Mama had cooked a big pot of chitterlings just for me. All my sisters and brothers and their children came, we had a stinky fest. I 'm thinking it was the Fourth of July because we had homemade ice cream also. This was the first time they had seen my son and mama thought he was the sweetest baby in the world. However, she was worried about how much he was spitting up. Every time I gave him a bottle he would throw it up. He had been doing this since the day he was born. I had taken him to several doctors and each time they would just change his formula. This wasn't helping. He was even throwing up the breast milk. My mama decided to take him to one of the doctors down there. He could not find anything wrong but told me to take him off the bottle and just breast feed until I go back to Houston. I had so much fun with my family.

I kept all the secrets about what was going on in my life bottled up inside of me.

Mama and my Aunt could not believe how much I had matured. They teased me about how I wasn't lazy anymore. I was washing dishes, folding clothes, cooking, and ironing and they did not have to beg me anymore.

Everywhere I went old friends went on about how my skin looked and how well I looked because I had lost so much weight. People really thought they were encouraging me but actually it was doing more damage. I couldn't help but think that everything my daddy and my husband had ever said about me must have been true. You know comments like, "You sure look a lot better than you use too," the intentions was good so I would just smile and say thank you. We really should be mindful of how we say things even when we mean good.

My mama and my Aunt kept telling me I was pregnant again and in my heart I knew I was but I didn't want to believe it, because my baby boy wasn't even four months yet. They were going on my radiant glow and my cotton white eyes. I wanted six children so badly and I wanted them close together but I didn't know if I wanted them this close. Some of my family suggested to me getting an abortion but this was totally out of the question. I asked my mama if she could give back one of her children or have an abortion which one would she choose. She knew she could not choose either one of us, so she said if you are pregnant have your baby and get your tubes tied. I knew I wasn't going to do that either because my heart was set on six children.

Well, sadly enough the week trip ended and it was time to go back home. I was so sad to say good-by to my mama-daddy and all my family but I knew I had too. I was even sadder to go back to the meanness and the abuse.

CHAPTER 8

A CLOSE CALL

WHEN WE MADE IT HOME I was glad to see my husband and acted as if though he was glad to see me. The next few weeks went by and everything was going well. He had a good job, all the bills were paid and the kitchen was full of food and better than anything we had not argued even one time. The pediatrician had changed the babies' formula again and he was still throwing up after each feeding. He was beginning to look weak and pale even the church members were noticing he looked very sick. My husband and I were becoming concerned but nothing was working.

It had now been confirmed that I was expecting my third child and although I was totally happy I didn't have total peace because my baby was sick. He could not keep down anything, not milk, cereal, juice or water.

Things were really looking bad. He wasn't crying at all although I knew he had to be hungry. The doctors were puzzled they could not find anything.

One night after my husband left for work I was sitting on the sofa with my baby boy lying on my lap. I was talking to one of the young ladies from church explaining to her how sick he was acting. She had a baby boy who was a week younger than my baby boy and at least three or four times bigger than him. She told me to get a spoon of mashed potatoes that we had for dinner and put just a little in his mouth. She wanted me to see if his stomach would tolerate it. Well, I tried that and in a matter of minutes he was vomiting worse than ever. This time he vomited until it turned into a yellowish, greenish liquid. I knew something was severely wrong. I called my husband at work and within a few minutes he came home and we went to the emergency room. His pediatrician came and was very disturbed. She knew my baby didn't have long to live but she didn't know why. She called in a stomach specialist but he too could not understand what was going on.

There was a young Chinese intern on call whom had examined the baby first and insisted that he felt a knot in his stomach, he asked permission to check him again. This time he felt the knot again but the doctors said it was nothing. He insisted to us that he felt the knot asking my husband and me to try and feel it. Fortunately, we felt the hard place and insisted that they did an x-ray on him. Immediately upon viewing the x-rays the specialist spotted the problem. He had a very rare disorder called intussusception, which meant his intestine had somehow went within itself, which caused his milk to come back up when he nursed. If you blew a balloon up a small amount and pushed your finger in it until it covered your finger this is what a large part of his intestine had done.

All the doctors came in and we immediately knew it wasn't good news. They explained what was going on using the balloon as an example. They gave him forty-eight hours to live without surgery and a fifty-fifty chance to live if he had the surgery. My husband was timid about making a decision and signing the forms. The doctor explained that the baby's life was in our hands. We had to choose to let him die in two days or to have the surgery and hope he lives. I signed the papers trusting God that I was making the right decision he was transferred to Texas Children Hospital where he had the surgery on the next day.

We sat in the waiting room for a couple hours when we received the call letting us know that the surgery had begun. Much to my surprise he insisted that we leave and go home, he wanted to have sex. My heart dropped! I started to cry, I could not believe he expected me to leave my baby and go home. "If you know what's good for you, you will leave now," he insisted. I did not want to make a big scene before everyone so I left. I remember crying all the way home and all through his love making. My mind was on my baby boy. When he was finished I took a bath and soon returned to the hospital. My little boy was out of surgery and already in his room. His frail little body was covered in tubes, the doctors explained they had to remove a portion of his intestines and the rest of the night would be very critical. He left with our little girl when visiting hour was over. I did not close my eyes all night. I sat there holding his tiny little hands praying God would let him live. Well, God answered my prayers and he's a healthy twenty-one year old today.

CHAPTER 9

HAVING BABY NUMBER THREE

AFTER MOVING TO OUR THIRD apartment things were still going downhill. I hated the apartment and was unhappy even more. It seemed he was mad at the world and taking it out on me. No matter how long or how hard I prayed the abuse continued. It was getting easier for him to hit me. I recall a specific day; as usual I would go at a certain time to check the mail. I finished cooking dinner and my daughter and I walked down to the mail room. There was a young man sitting at the pool. As we were about to pass by he spoke and told me, he admired me for how I always looked and how I kept my little girl looking so cute. I smiled and said thank you and kept walking. I did not know he was standing in the door watching me. Neither, did I think it was wrong to thank a person for such a nice compliment. When I was approaching the doorway he had already closed it and went inside. I put the mail on the table and started fixing the plates.

I called him to the table. I could tell he was upset about something but I didn't say anything. Soon I would know exactly what was bothering him. He asked what the man had said to me at the pool. I told him he said he admired me for fixing myself and our daughter up every day. He said I was lying the man had said more, he insisted. I knew not to say anything else because no matter what I said he would only get angrier. He took his hot plate of food and dashed it in my face, the plate fell and broke. He started beating me. My daughter grabbed the baby and ran in her room. I was pleading with him to stop and trying to protect my stomach at the same time. When everything was finally over, I cleaned the mess from the floor, fixed him some more food and sat there as if nothing had happened. This type thing went on constantly. The doctor was concerned that I was losing weight and not gaining but the baby was growing and developing on time. I wasn't getting out the apartment a lot. It was winter now and nearing my delivery date. I had our third little girl and a new hell began. It seemed that when I was losing weight during the pregnancy my baby had suffered the consequences. Water had been seeping from the water bag and the baby had developed a condition from a lack of oxygen which had literally burned her skin and darkened it, I had a very dry birth, but she was the easiest baby to be born. When he came to the hospital to see her he did not show any excitement.

We had every reason to be excited, not only had God blessed us with a beautiful baby girl, the doctor had pulled something off where we would not get a hospital bill. He even told me the eight hundred dollars we would owe him had been written off. Further in these chapters you will see somehow his miracle continued some months later.

We took our baby girl home three days later and new problems began. He had not ever once touched her; he'd just look at her and say, "She's not getting any lighter!" One day when she was about a month old he started saying she wasn't his. "She's too dark to be mine," he said this repeatedly.

We had a blood test done to prove she was his. I was humiliated to have to go through all of this. She looked just like my other two children she was just darker.

Even after proving she was his he didn't show any love to her and had not held her one time. One night I was cooking and trying to get some things done and the baby was crying out of control. I was tired. I begged him to hold her. He refused. He started hitting me and saying I'm not putting my hands on her. It was pouring down raining outside but I bundled all three of the children up and left the apartment. This time I had decided I was calling my parents to come and get me. I wasn't taking it anymore. I crossed the street and picked up the pay phone to call them collect. There I stood with three children, in a strange city, on a strange street in the pouring down rain, feeling like a poor boy a long ways from home. I could not do it, I could not call. I went back home with tears pouring down my face. I couldn't understand why it was happening but I didn't like it. I walked in the door he reached for the baby and took her in his arms for the first time. After that she became special in his sight and until this day he has treated her special.

Now, the tables have turned and he swears I have mistreated her because she's darker than the other children. I love all my children equally, I treat them all differently but fairly, all children are different so you can't possibly treat them the same. We were hurting more and more. Life was getting harder every day. Even having enough food to eat was a problem. Sometimes having milk for the two babies was next to impossible. There were days I had to breastfeed my son on one side and my little girl on the other side. Although my husband was working he wasn't making enough money to cover everything.

I remember one week it got especially tough on us. He had not received a paycheck. If memory serves me right he might have been laid off his job again. Every cabinet in the kitchen was bare; the refrigerator was next to empty. Lately, he had asked his relatives so much until we just did not want to ask again. It was Thursday and all we had left was a couple slices of beef liver a little salt and some collard greens that my mama had preserved for me, she cooked them and put them in a plastic container. I cooked half of what I had allowing my husband and the two older children to eat it. I made a sacrifice for them to eat and I went to bed hungry. All three of the children slept through the night. We went to bed knowing we would have a problem the next day.

Soon, morning came; we had no breakfast or anything. Before long the children was crying from being hungry. It was hard producing milk but I breastfed anyway. My son was a little over a year old and my baby was a few months. I believe the closeness they felt from being breastfed calmed them more than anything. My oldest daughter who was a little over three tried hard not to cry or ask for food. Somehow she understood what was going on. Later in the day I cooked the rest of the food and followed the same procedure as the day before.

The next day was absolutely awful. It was Saturday and by now the only thing left was a small amount of greens I had saved for my oldest daughter.

Well, now as the day went by she began to cry also. Her stomach was cramping from hunger pains. She remembers all of this and jokes often now that her stomach was so empty until when she had a bowel movement it was the pure collard greens in the toilet.

It had been three days since I had eaten anything and I was beginning to feel very weak myself. My daughter and I went to check the mail hoping and praying for a miracle but we didn't get one. The mail man was there and he had already passed our mailbox. We walked back to the apartment, I was passed disappointed. He had told me to get everyone dressed because if everything else failed he would ask his family to buy us some food. As we were about to leave the Holy Spirit spoke to me and said go check your mail box again. This was probably an hour later from the first time. I told him to wait a minute, I didn't tell him what the Spirit had said, I just told him that I was going to check the

mail again. This time I ran to the mail room. The mail man had returned and was about to drive off. I told him," I thought you left an hour ago." "Yes, I did but I realized I'd dropped a letter in my truck so I came back to put it in the mailbox."

I did not know who's mailbox he was talking about, but I knew this we had been praying for money, we were praying for a miracle and I knew God said, "Go check the mailbox again." I was shaking opening the mailbox there inside was an envelope. I was almost scared to touch it. I took it out and it was from an insurance company that we had when I was in my first trimester of pregnancy with my third child. However, my husband was off the job and we had been told they wouldn't pay for anything. Earlier in this chapter I told you, you would see another string the doctor had pulled for us, he wiped the hospital bills out the system, he did not charge us anything for my nine months of private care and now someway, somehow the money that would be owed to him he had fixed it where the insurance had to pay it but instead of taking it he had the check written out to us. We know it was from God but he used this doctor to give us a blessing. The check was close to a thousand dollars. I ran back to the apartment, tears pouring down my face, I was so overjoyed I couldn't say anything I just gave him the envelope. We all kneeled and thanked God for the miracle. That night we ate at one of my favorite seafood restaurants, bought everything we all needed and the next few weeks things were better. He was soon returned to work and believe it or not I was pregnant with my fourth child. My family and his had been so disappointed in us for having children close together until this time we kept it a secret that I was pregnant. Things were better financially with this baby we had our good insurance back and everything. I went back to the same doctor. He was very concerned about me being pregnant so often.

CHAPTER 10

HAVING BABY NUMBER FOUR

THE ABUSE CONTINUED THROUGHOUT THIS pregnancy. I recall this one time he was about to leave for work and I had forgotten to do something he had told me to do. I don't remember what it was but he became very angry about it. He was already dressed for work. I was apologizing about the matter and before I knew it he knocked me on the floor and just started punching me. I was in my seventh month and for the first time my stomach started hurting real bad. I was begging him to stop, stating I think something was wrong with the baby. He was yelling, "Do you think I care?" He was wearing steel toed boots and the last thing he did before- he left out the door. He kicked me on the left side of my stomach with those boots. I screamed to the top of my lungs it hurt so badly. In this apartment I had been beaten so many times. His favorite thing to hit me with was wooden handled jump ropes but never had he gone this far. He left as if though he had not done anything. The baby did not move for hours, I just knew she was dead. I prayed and cried hour after hour. A huge big puffy knot as big as a saucer was on my stomach. It was as blue as ink. I was beyond afraid. I kept praying that my baby was okay. Before morning I felt her kicking and knew she was okay. The bruise went away before my next office visit and when I was checked the baby was fine. It is amazing to me how God has the baby tucked away so safely inside the mother. He truly has kept me and my children.

After having my fourth daughter things were still going okay. We were still living in the apartment that I hated. It was cold in the winters and hot in the summer and they were refusing to fix anything. We were making plans to move to a bigger nicer place.

On an occasion we had gone over to one of his relatives home, I was never allowed at that time to get out and nor was the children. He drove up somewhere around three that evening, either a Saturday or a Sunday, this happened quite often because he would go over and watch football, while we sat in the car for endless hours. This particular day it was very cold and it seemed he forgot we were outside. We had no food, no way of using the restroom or anything. Around ten o'clock p.m. I just had simply had enough, the children was tired, hungry, and cold, we were restless and it just was wrong for him to leave us sitting there all that time. I never understood why he just would not leave us at home.

I don't know what made me do this. What gave me the nerves but I blew the horn three or four times. Finally, the owner came outside to see what was going on. He could not believe we had been sitting in the car for six or seven hours in the cold. This was not the first time this had happened. It had happened several times before he just never knew it. He talked about him so bad for what he had done. He got in the car and drove away. At first he didn't say anything. He made it to the end of the street; he got out and got the car jack, "I'm going to kill you tonight! You embarrassed me! You made me look bad!" he said. I was trying to get out but he had me locked in, I was begging him not to hit me with the jack. Somehow he put the jack down and drove off, threatening to kill me when we got home. I was pleading with him, telling him how sorry I was for embarrassing him. "I can't wait until I get home to hurt you," he said.

He drew his fist back and hit me in my left eye with all his might. For a minute everything went black, I was in shock; I didn't know how to act or what to say I just started screaming from the agonizing pain. I was holding my hand over my eye screaming. People in their cars were looking but they didn't do anything. He kept telling me to shut up but I just could not. He took his fist and this time hit me in the mouth busting my top lip open. Blood was pouring out. What was he doing to me? I didn't understand. I can't make you know how I was hurting from the pain and for how he was hitting me in my face. I remember thinking this is my face, what is he doing to my face. I got home and I knew I had more pain coming. I put the children to bed. My oldest daughter was looking at me she wanted to cry so badly. She just held to me while I was undressing everyone for bed. She could see what I had not seen yet. I sat in the room with them and in a few minutes they all had fallen asleep.

Finally, I built my nerves to go in the restroom. I could feel the puffiness around my eye and my lip was so swollen I could not close it, it hurt so badly. When I looked in the mirror I panicked. "Oh God, God what did he do to me! Look, what you did! Look what you did, I said.

I didn't care if he hit me again. I wanted him to know how I felt. He couldn't even look at me and for some unknown reason he couldn't finish what he had started. The next morning I woke up with a black eye. He went to the store and bought things to try to make up for what he had done. No flowers, candy, or even diamonds could make me feel better. My face was messed up for the next two weeks. This would be the first of at least three or four black eyes and busted lips while being married to him.

There are some of you going through this right now. There are preacher's wives and other women reading this book through black eyes right now, God do not want you living like this. Please find a safe way of escape. You are more than the abuse. You do not deserve to be mistreated. Love yourself enough to help yourself.

I can tell you because I know what years of abuse will eventually do to you. It eats away at the inner person in you. Quit protecting your husband while killing yourself daily. Getting out will help him and you more than staying in this situation.

I can't find a word that would allow you to know how it feels to be a grown lady and yet to be treated like a child. This beating had affected me in a whole new way. It had gone further than the others. I had to miss church, bible class, could not go on my daily walks or anything. I was confined to the house until every visible scar was healed. I had to protect his image. I could not nor would not let people know he was this kind of monster. I was beginning to conceal more and more secrets.

Over the next few weeks things was pretty calm. I spent many nights alone and afraid while he worked the grave yard shift. The three youngest children were always in the bed at seven o'clock, but the oldest would be awake for hours before she'd finally fall asleep. It's like she knew the pain I was feeling and she wanted to make me feel better.

The days of abuse was taking its toll on me. I found comfort in caring for my children, I found joy in doing all I could to make him happy, but I found my peace late at night when everyone was sleeping. I would read the bible for hours. I found strength, hope, and courage in all the books of Psalms. I had closeness with God, I took this time to pray, to talk to him. Yes, I knew all the rules that people say, don't ask God why. Well, I broke the rules. I asked why all the time. What had I done that caused me to have to suffer in such a way? I'd been around my family all my life and none of my nieces and nephews had ever gone hungry, or had no toys or anything. I questioned God often, Why me? I never received an answer but I never felt God loved me any less. I've received all my answers now and I know it was all about you, my readers.

There was days in this apartment when I would run outside on the patio as I was being beat. I knew he would not hit me outside. He had only hit me once on the freeway with cars passing by. Most abusers are cowards they do their dirty work behind closed doors.

I remember some days sitting on the patio for hours in the cold or the heat. I felt like a caged animal. He would lock every door so I couldn't get back in. My children would sit behind the curtains playing and watching me for hours. He would eventually come and open the door and I would go on with my task. Running and hiding had become a part of my life. Whether it was closets, bathrooms, or the patio I would hide there. The abuse continued sometimes on a daily basis. I realize now that inside of that cowardly person that did such awful things to me was a child like person who needed love and attention. I guess that's why on most occasions he wanted sex after all his anger. I realize now that he did not know how to love, how to nourish and how to cherish. Even in my trying to do all that I thought was right somehow I too was making mistakes.

We talk a lot now that we are a part how we let things and people come between us. We know that was not all the problem but it was some. For the most part throughout our marriage everything was about our children, especially as they became teenagers. I began to hang out more and more with them and less with him. He admits now that he was very jealous of my closeness to our children. The years of neglect and abuse caused me to grow and bond with them even more. With them I could be myself, I could be silly and witty, I could laugh, I could cry, I was never ashamed to eat in front of them, I was not ashamed of my dress size with them, they had become my motivation to live. I ventured away from the chapter a little to tell you to always make time for one another.

Communication is the key. In all the years of abuse we never once talked about what it was doing to me, it's like we swept it under the rug and kept it a big family secret.

Well, a few months have passed and we have moved to a bigger apartment. This time I love it; this apartment was as big as a house, three bedrooms. He bought new furniture for most of the rooms, I had plants everywhere. He never bought me roses but he bought me plants all the time. Again, I was hoping life would be better here.

CHAPTER 11

HAVING BABY NUMBER FIVE

I WAS PREGNANT WITH MY fifth child and beyond happy because we had been told we were having a boy. My oldest daughter has started pre-K and loves it. She loved going to school and could not wait for me to walk her every morning. I met a few ladies and we would walk together and even sometimes do some window shopping across the street.

On Saturdays sometime the girls and I would spend the entire day at the mall. For the most part I never had any money but I didn't mind it was just a delight to be among all the people. Most of the couples would be holding hands and smiling, you could literally feel the love coming from them. On occasions people would ask to buy candy or treats for my daughters and on rare occasions I'd scrap change to have money for treats. There was even a few times when he would give me money to spend.

Sometimes when things had been especially hard on me I would go alone or only take my oldest daughter. You would be surprised how much better you feel just to get away from problems if only for a few hours.

This is how I got back in touch with a friend I'd known since I was six years old. She worked at a drug store behind the mall. I would always walk to it to meet my husband to go back home.

Most Saturdays he took our son for a burger or something and went home to watch sports.

On occasions he found things to kick me around for. He had gotten where he would scratch me real bad on my arms and sometimes in my chest. One day one of the ladies at my church noticed a scratch on me and asked me if he did it. I made up something and she went on. Thinking about it now I realize you become a liar also because you lie to cover up for the abuser.

I started babysitting two ladies' children in the complex. I was able to keep this money for myself. It felt so good to have a few dollars of my own. He tried to buy things I needed but I just wanted sometimes to see things I wanted and get them.

Late one night he had beat me so badly until I was screaming for my life. I don't recall what it was about. I tried to go to bed afterward but he poured water on my side of the bed. I would be too afraid to try to sleep somewhere else so I slept in the wet spot. This happened on many occasions. The next morning we were walking our children to school and the lady who lived above us said she needed to talk to me. I kept her daughter for her so I assumed it was about that. She walked back and when we were alone she asked me was he beating me. She told me how they would hear me screaming at night and how they could hear the licks. She said the next time she heard something she was going to call the police. I begged her not to. I assured her that nothing was what she thought it was. I told her he threw things when he was angry and that's all she was hearing. She had been abused by her first husband. She had a very bad heart and could not stand a lot of trauma. She pleaded with me to leave him and she would help me. This reminded me of an occasion in the last apartment when we had argued and I tried to leave.

I called a shelter and they sent a cab for me. I packed a few necessities for me and my four children and prepared to leave. We were on our way to bible class one Sunday evening when all hell broke loose. As we were driving down one of the neighborhood streets we noticed three young ladies walking down the street. He was very attracted to high light skinned people. One of them was a very light skinned beautiful young lady. They were all dressed in skimpy clothing. He stared at her so hard until he hit the curb.

He was so embarrassed. The first words out of his mouth were, "I was not lusting!"

I had not accused him of anything, yet, I sure was thinking it.

He felt bad for what he had done so he picked a fight with me. He said he would take care of me after bible class. When class was over we immediately left.

You would think he would have heard something in class that would have changed his mind about his intention but it never happened. If he said I'm going to get you, just like when your parents said that to you, you could depend on it.

This night evolved into something that was unbelievable even to me. I had kept silent through the whole ordeal but then I asked him was he guilty of lust the reason he was so mad. He hit me across the face knocking me to the wall. He went mad; he said things about me that I can't repeat, comparing me to the young lady from the street as to why he'd rather look at her. This night was so different. He called his mother and mine. He told his mother he was going to kill me. Again, he told my parents to come get me and if memory serves me right they arrived on the next day.

This was a never ending fight it went on and on. I was beyond tired. I was tired in every imaginable way. I took so many punches in the head, so many kicks to the back of my legs, until I was trembling all over. I hollered until I had no voice left. The more he hit me the angrier he became. For a minute he left the room. Something came over me. I knew if I didn't do something he was going to kill me.

I picked up the phone and dialed 911. I was only able to say help me. He caught me on the phone, I quickly hung it up, but the police called back. He snatched the cord out the wall but in a matter of minutes they were knocking on the door.

The abuse was apparent, I had scratches everywhere, my clothes was ripped, hair messed up and everything.

They wanted to arrest him but I would not press charges. The lady officer gave me a number to a shelter and the first chance I got I called them. I packed some things and waited for the cab to arrive.

When the cab arrived I got my four children and my suitcase and walked out the door. I was so scared I was shaking. I didn't have anyone to call; I had no idea what I was doing. I put my two youngest daughters in the car and as soon as I reached for my son and other daughter he grabbed them. I begged him to give me my children but he would not. They were crying to the top of their voice. I had to make a choice. I was yelling from the cab saying "Mama will be back tomorrow for you!" The cab driver drove away, I was crying out of control, he was running after the cab and my babies was screaming, "Mama, Mama! Come back!" The cab driver said, "Mam I can't do this, go back and try to work it out!"

He put the car in reverse, helped get my daughters and the suitcase out and drove away.

I just knew life was really over for me then, I was walking to the apartment begging him to please don't hit me again. I hugged my children and sit in their room until they fell asleep. I took a bath and went to bed. We ended the dreadful night with sex as usual.

The next morning I could barely drag my hurting body out of bed. My parents made their third and final trip to Texas. I never once called my parents to come get me. My parents vowed they would never waste time again coming when he called.

I could not tell my neighbor this story because it would have been admitting what she suspected. She said as long as we were neighbors she was going to look out for me.

I went home and told him that the neighbors had heard him hitting me. I told him they said if they heard noise again they would call the police.

This did not mean much to him. The abuse continued and they never called the police.

We now have five children and life isn't easy. On occasions we still have singing engagements and crusades and the money is always a blessing. A church member convinced me to get WIC and that saves a bundle. The free baby milk, milk, cereal, eggs and cheese saved us over a hundred dollars in food.

CHAPTER 12

STARTING A NEW BUSINESS

CHURCH MEMBERS ASKED ME TO make socks and hair bows for their daughters like the ones I made for my daughters. They looked better than the ones from the store. My mother and sisters had been encouraging me to sale them. Before I could blink my eyes this became a booming business. Most weeks just the orders my sister got on her job in Mississippi exceeded three hundred dollars.

For a few months this became our only source of income. He had been hurting for months in his shoulder. He thought it was from lifting boxes every night. However, he soon discovered after seeing several doctors he had cracked a bone in his shoulder. It could not be fixed so they had to remove it. He put the surgery off as long as he could. He was off work for days and soon we were back in a financial strain. Bills were piling up and the money was getting less and less. Once again the kitchen cabinets were getting bare. One day he had took the children out riding and looking at vehicles. He knew he couldn't afford anything but they went looking anyway.

I stayed home to have some time to myself and make merchandise as well. I started thinking about my life and before I knew it I was sobbing out of control. There I sat in my late twenties, with a husband that did not love me and five beautiful innocent children whom had suffered their whole lives. It seems as if someone had wished a curse on us and sometimes I believe they had. I was watching one of the Christian networks (The Oasis of Love) they had a number flashing across the screen. I dialed the number and requested prayer. The lady on the other end not only prayed but she prophesied. She encouraged me to move all pride and go and get food stamps so we would always have food. She told me God was going to do something supernatural to prove to me that he had not forgotten about us. She gave me the number to the welfare office. When I hung up I called and made an appointment. He had never wanted any government assistance and neither did I. He had made an exception about WIC so I had hope he would do the same about the food stamps.

He came home in a new custom van which had a colored television and everything in it. I couldn't say anything although I knew we couldn't afford it, I knew this was the supernatural blessing. We also needed it because it was impossible to fit five car seats in our Lincoln.

He agreed for me to keep the appointment and things were better as far as food was concerned.

The bills were still not being paid on time. We had to make partial payments on rent in order to pay other bills. Soon, things just got completely out of hand. Our lights were turned off. We were living in a total electric apartment. This meant no hot water, no television, and no place to keep the food cold. This was not a temporary thing it lasted almost three months.

I was forced to measures that I would never even dream of. One day while getting the mail he discovered an electrical outlet on the side of our apartment which was a part of the complex. That is to say it was for the use of the maintenance people. We had a big heavy duty extension cord so every night when he left for work, I'd go outside, sneak and plug the cord and run it into our apartment. We had a hot plate, so I would cook food, heat water for hot baths, and on occasions turn on the television.

More and more I was beginning to feel like a bum. I felt like we were going through hell and I kept it a secret, I was too ashamed to tell any of my family. On occasions the neighbors would mock us by unplugging the cord, knocking on the door, and bursting out with laughter. My oldest daughter and I would wait until they leave and go out and plug it again. Sometimes they would do it late at night and we would just leave it off. I never remember him, even on weekends humiliating his self-doing this.

I was so tired of living like that stealing electricity, keeping our food in an ice chest, and taking small baths. There we sat in a big beautiful apartment living in terrible conditions.

Several nights' people tried to break in. On one occasion a young man who worked at a nearby grocery store almost got in. I called him to come home. The police were already there when he came. They told him the danger he was letting his family live in to be there with no electricity. They gave us a number to call the next day to get help getting our lights on. At this complex drug dealing was becoming rapid. We had been living there over a year now and had been considering moving. On occasions there were times we literally saw bullets flying in front of our windows. All of this mixed with our problems, we made a decision if the people chose to help we would move back to the original area we had lived in when I first moved to Texas.

On the next day we got dressed and went to the place to get help on the bill. I was on unusual turf but as years passed it became familiar ground, I was standing in help lines more than I should have been. I thought we would go to one place and that would be it, but, no it becomes a cycle. They send you from one place to the next. I felt like yesterday's garbage. Actually, from where I came from I thought this was beneath me. My husband sat in the van at every place, supposedly keeping the children. Personally, I think he was too embarrassed to get out.

Finally, all these places combined got the three hundred dollar light bill paid. We had the lights turned on in our new apartment. It was even nicer than the last one. Within a few weeks his pain was so severe until he had to have surgery. The next few months would prove to be very critical financially. It took some time for him to get his workers compensation. We managed to keep our bills paid and with the food stamps we were always full.

We were not able to get out and sale many bows because of his pain.

We started making plans to buy a home. We were both tired of the constant moving. His workers compensation would be settled in a few weeks and we were going to use some of the money as a down payment. We checked the paper every day for available homes. We wanted a backyard for the children to play in and just a place that felt like home.

The holidays came and were more special this year than ever. When we had to go to the different charities they had us to sign a list for Christmas gifts. On Christmas Eve they brought boxes of gifts and food. He had also bought them lots of toys as well. We had not really celebrated Christmas together. The church we attended did not believe it was necessary to exchange gifts.

Christmas has always been my favorite time of the year and although I know it's not about the gifts it still feels good, both to give and receive. I remember feeling happy and joyous most of the day. We called our families and they were all happy. Knowing how happy they all were made me even happier.

It was a joy to watch the children riding their new hot wheels, playing with dolls and other toys. For a few hours at least, life seemed normal and it felt good to be on one accord. We did not have many arguments or fights the six months we lived here. Most days I had to get up early and walk the children to school. We had three in school now. It felt good to get out and walk every day. I would also take the youngest two in the double stroller just to get them out the house. Except for the mornings the dogs would be roaming the streets we'd have a blast every morning. Some evenings if we had extra money we would eat ice cream at the Dairy Queen located nearby we lived.

Some evenings I'd sat on the steps of our building and watch them play at the playground. Seeing our children running and playing made me want a house even more.

Things worked out with the workers compensation. We put a down payment on a beautiful home, paid off some bills, had fun eating out and buying things we all needed and even saved for a rainy day.

Well, our six month lease was up on our apartment and our house wasn't ready for us to move in. The owner was having the walls painted and new carpet and appliances put in. His relatives suggested we live with them until they got our house ready. We put all our things in storage and lived with them a few months. Weekday's we would take the children to school and go to the park and stay until they got out of school.

After a few days this became very tiresome. Sometimes I felt like we were wearing out our welcome. We made it a practice to be gone as much as possible, and stay confined in our one room if possible.

I cooked dinner every evening, helped with homework, and continued designing socks and hair bows for my special customers.

Once again our lives was about to be turned upside down. He had been talking about moving back to Mississippi, however not to our hometowns. I had a lot of mixed feeling and emotions about this situation. A move had been on his mind for a few years. He felt as an Evangelist God was leading him this way. Several months before deciding to move here he talked about it more and more. We had what seemed to be more than our share of problems and for the first time in our marriage things were looking up, or at least it looked that way. We were at the end of our rent to own lease, the next payment we would be buying our first home, a beautiful home in a quiet suburban area. I loved this house it was perfectly landscaped. One of my greatest joys was when I could take a break from the business and work in my flower garden. I found a lot of peace in watching my children run and play in the front yard while I tended the flowers. Sometimes it actually seemed as though life was perfect for those few hours. This house was more than I'd ever really hoped for. I guess the living room was my favorite, in my opinion it was perfectly decorated and the cathedral ceilings were a dream. He had his faults but one thing I can say when it came to furniture he bought me everything I wanted. My daughters had white canopy beds in their room, with matching desk, dressers and chest with all yellow decorations, this was my second favorite room. How could I move? For some reason a lot of my memories are faded the year we lived here. I guess it's because my life was so busy. The designers socks and hair bow business was keeping me up for days at a time. Most nights I wasn't getting any sleep at all. I wanted so much to be home and enjoy it. I had a new king size bedroom that I very seldom was sleeping in. The demand for my merchandise was getting to be too much for me. He still wasn't working and was helping me as much as he could. We had our merchandise in over five children's stores. We had to meet the demand of all those contracts plus our personal customers. The money was looking good. Soon he found a job and went back to work, then I was doing all the work by myself but at least I was at home more. On Saturdays we made deliveries to our personal customers which was an all day job and most time half the night. I don't recall making less than four or five hundred dollars on Saturdays alone.

I was so tired and worn out until moving was beginning to sound okay. He was having a really hard time deciding what to do. As I said things was looking up for us financially. On his days off he would make deliveries to the stores while I stayed home and continued sewing. Between cooking, cleaning, homework, dressing children and the business I was at the edge of collapsing. I guess I'll never forget the day he came in with a $1500.00 order from a Jewish lady who owned the biggest children store in Houston. She wanted us to sign a contract with her that would start at $1500.00 and guaranteed to double to $3000.00 a month the next month. This was our biggest contract yet, the others were running between three and five hundred monthly. This was great we could be making five thousand or more a month. We discussed letting some of the stores go in order to meet her demand. Soon, we were thinking maybe we should put off moving. We went all over trying to get a loan to meet the demands of this contract; it seemed God closed every door. We could not get a penny anywhere. He was even laid off his job. Early one morning very unexpectedly the man that owned our house knocked on the door and gave us a thirty day notice to move out. He had no explanation just that he decided not to sell the house. In a matter of hour's things was plummeting downhill. As days went by some of the stores began to order less and less and even our personal customers was buying less.

It seemed as if God was pulling the rug from under us. His mind began to focus back on God telling him to move from this city. As I said, I had mixed feelings about moving. I felt life had been tough for us before but we always bounced back, what was different about this time. However, he was convinced we were not going to bounce back from this fall. According to him this was God's way of convincing us to move. Thinking over the way my marriage had been the last few years I did not want to be anywhere near my family. I did not want them knowing about the abuse, or the hard time we might go through but more than anything I did not want them to think I wanted their sympathy or support in anyway. All my life I had heard if you make your bed hard you have to lay in it. I hated the thought of coming to Mississippi. He had not fully made a decision but suggested that I start packing anyway. I remember crying as I packed boxes of dishes, towels, sheets and you get the picture. One day while packing someone knocked on the door. It was a good friend of his whom was a fireman and a preacher. He'd stopped by to ask for prayer for a Hispanic family that had come to his church. It seemed they had nothing and had been living in a horse stable. The church had found them a home to live in but they had no furniture. For a week I had been calling storage units trying to find some place to put our furniture and it seemed every place in the yellow pages was full. It seemed God had closed yet another door. After the preacher left my husband came in went in the bedroom and continued to pray. Several hours later he came out with words I'll never forget. He told me what the preacher had said and then he said, "I feel that's why we can't find storage God wants us to give everything away." I was shocked and hurt at first and asked him if he was sure. We had never met this family and still never met them but I told him to do what he felt God wanted him to do. He said I'm going to bless at least three families. That weekend we had a crusade in Beaumont, Texas which was Halloween weekend of 1990. The pastor invited us over to his house he had a wife and four children. They did not have a lot at all, immediately we knew this was the second family we were going to bless. Their television set was old and the picture was very frosty and they had a picnic table for a dining table. After the crusade we had planned to go back to Houston for a week and then move to Mississippi. Again our plans changed. My children and I stayed in Beaumont while my husband and the pastor went back to our home in Houston. Before leaving for Beaumont we had given our next door neighbors probably three months' worth of grocery, everything in our pantry and freezer. They had a baby so we also gave them baby strollers, clothes and other things. After returning to Houston, my husband, the pastor from Beaumont and the fireman preacher got together and divided the furniture. The fireman needed a bedroom suit for his two daughters, so he took the canopy bedroom suit and all the accessories for them along with the freezer. The pastor took the television, dining table, chairs, china cabinet, sheets, towels, etc. They gave the Mexican family, the living room set, tables, lamps, curtains, two bedroom suits and the dishes, pots and kitchen stuff was divided among the pastor and the Mexican family.

After returning to Beaumont the only things packed in our custom van were our clothes which were the only things we kept. Some clothes were given to the Salvation Army. My husband pawned the sewing machine for extra money to get to Mississippi. Out of all the things that we gave up I was more concerned about the flowers. Much to my surprise several of the neighbors had asked for them dug them up and planted them in their yards. We spent a few days in Beaumont with our new found friends. I will never forget this family. We brought so much joy in their life. The pastor took my husband the next day to a place that put new tires on our vehicle at no charge. They filled the van with gas at no charge and told us when we get to the city to go to this church (white members) in Pearl and they would give us money for a hotel.

CHAPTER 13

MOVING TO MISSISSIPPI

WELL, THE DECISION HAD BEEN made and we were on our way to Mississippi. It seemed as if hours turned into days traveling here. I felt so scared. I was terribly afraid I was coming to a strange place and he had made a decision not to tell our families we were in Mississippi. Nothing could have prepared me for this. First of all we were homeless, homeless with five children ranging in ages from three to nine. My greatest fear was that somehow my family would know I was being abused. I wanted my secret to remain a secret and living hundreds of miles apart was the best way to do that. The children slept most of the way. I guess they were too young to be afraid. They had already faced some difficult times in their short lives but compared to what was coming, life had been a piece of cake. Somewhere in my mind I had hope that life would be better here, I thought, well, it will be hard at first but then things will get much better.

Our first stop back in Mississippi was at a rest area. We stopped to use the restroom and walk around to relax our legs. I looked at my children running around in the grass as I sat at one of the park tables and thought how good it must have felt to them just to be young, free and not a problem in the world to deal with.

We arrived to the place we would call home about midday, tired, hungry and sleepy. He drove around looking for churches that might be open. Ironically, we went to a church that was having the Baptist Association meeting. We entered in and sat in the back of the church. My husband talked to some of the preachers in charge. They invited us to eat lunch with them. They asked us to come back that night and allow the children to sing. He was hoping they would give us money for a hotel but they did not. We had been instructed in Beaumont, Texas to go to this church in Pearl, Mississippi and tell them who we were, why we were here and tell them the person's name that sent us there. After doing so they gave us a check to pay for a hotel for a week.

On the way to the hotel we stopped at a gas station to get gas. Something took place there and I don't remember all the details so I can't paint you a complete picture. It seems my husband wanted me to spend food stamps to get change to help out on the gas money. I remembered being embarrassed and timid about going in. I told him I just could not do this. In times past I had to do this but I just could not in a strange place. You see you go in buy something and add it up making sure you would have change left over out of a dollar food stamp. I refused to get out the van and as much as I remember, he became very angry and frustrated. My worst nightmare came true, my question was answered. Would he abuse me here in my home state? Would I run if he did? Would I call my family? What would I do? He took his fist and hit me in the nose. I was wearing a light colored dress, I recall the gush of blood covering the front of my dress and then blood dripping from my nose. My children were screaming Daddy! Daddy! Please don't hit my mama. Mama's bleeding! He rushed away from the station before anyone could see what he had done. I can't express to you what I was feeling. All my hopes for a new beginning here had ended the first few hours of being here. I realize he was scared in the wrong way. He was a trembling coward that did not know how to deal with pressure. I walked in the hotel still bleeding both from my nose and my heart. The children wanted to rush to my aid but we all had learned not to react in his presence. I went in the restroom and cleaned myself up while he unloaded the clothes out the van. He instructed me to start getting ready for church that night. My mind wasn't on church; it wasn't on singing I just wanted to take a bath and go to sleep.

Again, I had to act as if nothing had happened and therefore, I started getting everyone dressed! We wore our black polka dotted dresses, and the boys wore black suits, crisp white shirts and black polka dotted bowties. The girls' hair was combed to perfection. We arrived at church promptly. No one, I mean not anyone would have suspected I'd just been punched in the nose. We sung two selections and after which was invited to churches all over the city. The president of the organization informed my husband that they would not help us in anyway but they would pray for us.

Over a period of time some of the preachers helped us quite a lot. Before we knew it our week at the hotel was almost over and we did not have money to continue staying there. On Sunday evening he said to me that God was leading him to a certain church that he attended when he was a student at Jackson State University. Well, we went there. They had a new pastor. He was young and very receptive of us. My husband told him why we were here and that he was an Evangelist and God sent us here. I know some of you have a problem believing God was speaking to him at all because of his behavior. However, I believe God speaks to us all and gives us all choices and opportunities but it's left to us how we deal with them.

The pastor gave us money for hot food and informed us he would stop by the hotel on the next day. I don't know how I knew it but somehow I knew he was going to help us. That night I slept better than I had in days. On the next day he arrived with more hot food for us came in an acted as if he had known us his whole life. He hugged all the children, me, and my husband. Somehow his presence made me feel things was going to be alright. It felt like God had sent someone to take care of us. He paid for us to stay in the hotel another week. We went back to his church on Sunday morning and the Mississippi hospitality shown through from most of his members.

Some of the ladies later became friends of mine.

The next Monday he came by the hotel to tell us God had informed him that he was the person to help us. He explained to us that he had a place for us to live, he said it wasn't fancy, wasn't in the best of shape but if we were willing to live there we could. He owned a body shop where he restored wrecked vehicles and he and his family had lived in this mobile home for years until God blessed them with a beautiful two story home.

CHAPTER 14

LIVING IN A CONDEMNED TRAILER

WHEN WE DROVE UP TO the home I must admit, my heart dropped in the bottom of my stomach. I was thinking it's no way we can live here. It was worse than I could have ever imagined. The windows were broken, the front door was off the hinges and propped up with an old dining room table, the kitchen floor had a huge hole in it. The bathrooms were clean but yet scary, there were three bedrooms, one of which was locked, the other was empty but I knew my children would never sleep in it. The back door was on the hinges but did not lock. I know it looks bad he explained but its shelter. My husband accepted his offer and for two years this was home. We ran extension cords from his shop to the refrigerator and to the one drop light we had from his shop.

The first night I was too afraid to sleep in there so we slept outside in our van.

Different churches helped us get the utilities connected and although this house was condemned by the city it became home. One of the preachers from the church gave us bunk beds for the children. We put them up in what used to be the living room, the three girls slept in one bed and the two boys in the other.

We slept in the bedroom next to the living room. We had two mattresses stacked together on the floor. We all slept this way for two years. We went from sleeping comfortably in a king size bed to a mattress on the floor. In these two years I never once heard my children complain about anything and for the most part if you ask them they'll tell you above everything these two years shaped us into the Christians we are now. Life wasn't easy but it was bearable. The three older children were enrolled in school. They soon made new friends and we all went on with life as normal as possible.

We had sad occasions and happy ones or at least funny ones. I think the most things in the world that I'm afraid of are mice/rats, you get the picture. This old trailer had no shortage of them. Some nights I would lay awake listening to them chewing inside the walls. My biggest fear was that one would crawl on my face if I fell asleep. There was one in particular we all remember. My children called him the holy rat. Each morning and night as we had our time of prayer and devotion to God this little mouse would sit in the corner of the front doorway and as soon as we were finished with devotion he'd leave. I had two awful experiences with them. Every morning when it was cold I'd get up early and turn on the oven on the stove and open the door to warm the house before my children woke up for school. Needless to say the mice had the same idea. I did not know they would gather around the pilot light to keep warm. As I opened the door three mice scoured around in the oven. No one on our street needed alarms that morning, I'm sure my screaming woke up the whole neighborhood. That was the last time I ever opened the door on the oven. No more biscuits, cakes, cornbread as long as we lived there. My children laughed for days about this so did my husband. On another occasion someone had left a bowl of water on the kitchen cabinet as I was about to pour it down the sink I noticed what I thought was a piece of meat so I took it out with my hand, as I did it started to crawl in the palm of my hand as I looked closer I noticed it was a small little baby mice. Even now my head is crawling just thinking about it.

I froze in my tracks, I could not move and I could not drop it, I screamed with everything within me. My husband ran out, he already knew I must have seen a mouse. He took it out of my hand and killed it. As I stood shaking and crying, he and the children stood laughing.

In spite of being hungry, sick, broke, and everything nothing was as bad as these experiences. I guess these things happened to bring some laughter in the home. One day the pastor who owned the trailer was inside eating dinner with my husband. My oldest daughter, who was maybe nine or ten at the time, was taking a bath when a mouse ran in the restroom where she was, she ran through the house butt naked screaming for her life. I guess we all laughed the rest of the day.

You know times were tough but for the most part we didn't let anyone or anything take our joy. Some days he could be sensible and others he was not.

Sometimes the days seemed as if they would never end. He would be gone somewhere with the pastor or working outside with him. My younger two children and I were stuck there alone. I would read scriptures to them from the bible teach them different things and after their naps they would play until the others would come home. After they completed their homework they would go outside and play. It was so amazing to me, they did not have one toy and every child on the street had bikes and most everything they desired but instead of playing with their toys they would come and play with my children. I said I would not discuss my children a lot in the book but this I must talk about because it opens the next part of our life.

Since my oldest son was two years old he'd been trying to preach. In the yard, my son would take old car tires and stack them up to make an altar to preach behind. He and his sister and brothers would sing and the other children would sit on the ground, listening and clapping. My son would sing Amazing Grace and then he would preach. I guess he was six and this continued week after week. After becoming born again himself he started asking the other children if they wanted to be saved and they would pray and become born again. The old man that lived next door would just stand under the tree and watch him. My son would get in trouble at school for preaching in the back of the classroom. He would tell his daddy everyday how much he wanted to preach in a real church. The pastor encouraged my husband to let him preach and at eight years old, in front of a packed church, he preached his first sermon.

By now our secret was revealed and our family was aware we were living in Mississippi. They had gone about some underhanded sneaky ways to find out. I remember feeling hurt when my mother called me one day asking me was it true that we were living under a bridge. I did not understand the laughter I heard in the background as she asked me. I know they had been upset with me having so many children and maybe somehow they thought I deserved this! The day came that my mother explained a lot of things to me. I would not have loved her any less either way.

Many opportunities were happening for my son to preach all over the state of Mississippi. We would go places where we were treated like queens and kings only to come back home to a condemned trailer not a palace. Well, now it was getting so hard for me, I wanted to get out of that trailer. The walls were closing in on me. Being around others and seeing how they were living was making reality set in on me. Again, I pretty much kept my thoughts to myself. I was hurting inside. I felt like a bum and degraded. I thought, "Why is this happening to us?" God was letting us have the best on Sundays but then the rest of the week, I thought, we were living in hell. I did not, refused to complain, I had to allow myself to think God had not forgotten about us. When you are going through heartaches and pains please know that God knows it, he sees it, he's even permitting it. I can assure you he will bring you out. He will not fail you. I didn't know then it was alright to be afraid, to be hurt, and to want a better life. I truly thought that wanting better meant I was losing faith, I wasn't trusting God. I know now it's okay to have a bad moment but then we are to pull ourselves up and just trust God.

I had days when I was still being hit on even through all of this. I had some very sick days while living in the trailer. I think I was stressed a lot. I put on a lot of weight as well.

I recall a Saturday night in particular. We had been invited to a church in our neighborhood to sing. This day had been one of those very hard days. We had no money or food, the children was extremely hungry and I had nothing to give them and no one to call for help. We had prayed most of the day but God had not sent a breakthrough. That night we got dressed and showed up for the program. My children were weak and hungry but they still sung and they did the best they could under the circumstances. However, their best was not good enough for their daddy. When we made it home he called them in the room and started fussing. He took off his belt and in a rare occasion he started to whip them for what he called messing up. He whipped the two youngest girls first and they came out the room crawling on the floor. I sat in the corner crying when I looked up to see my hungry, helpless babies lying there. I told them to never let anyone make them crawl like dogs. I picked them up and put them in the bed. As I did this something happened inside of me, I ran in the room and I grabbed the other three. I refused to let him hit them, I told them to crawl in their beds. This definitely was not the first time I stood up for my children and it would not be the last time. However, it was something different about this night. My children were frail, they were hungry and they didn't have a dog gone thing to do with it. They did not ask to be born into a life of hell and they did not sing poorly intentionally. He started raging, he became extremely angry. He was totally out of control. Before I knew it he grabbed me and threw me to the floor. I didn't scream. I knew the windows were broken and I did not want anyone to hear what was going on. We were known throughout the state as the holy family and in spite of all this my children and I tried our best to live to please God. I was wrong; God does not want us to stay in abusive, deadly situations, whether we are married to a preacher or a sinner. Hear this again, get out! GET OUT! GET OUT!

He beat me this night with the belt and his fist until I lost consciousness. I can honestly say to the best of my knowledge I died this night. I remember my head going blank and everything went black. As this was happening I could hear him saying, "You made me kill you; now my name is going to be drugged out in the news and everything, you made me kill you."

By now, I'm no longer in this world; I'm somewhere else in a world of peace and quietness. I guess I was in this state of mind for a few hours. He thought I was dead so he left, leaving me there with my five children. I thank God for my five children who believed in the power of praying. I don't know how they did it but they laid me on the mattress on the floor, they got the anointed oil, and instead of crying and screaming they poured the oil all over me and they prayed and begged God until he brought me back. I opened my eyes to five of the most perfect little faces in the world. I was so sore from being hit on. Then they were free to cry and they cried until they fell asleep on the mattress with me. Later that night he came back with bags of burgers and fries. I know now what I didn't know then. He was afraid; he felt worthless; he too was afraid and did not know how to deal with pressure. It took me years to figure this out. Preachers are supposed to be perfect, they are to never doubt God, but I know differently they are human just like you and me. They get scared, they sin, they cuss, they lie, and they fight. I find that when we are afraid we react in different ways, some cry, some smoke, some over eat, some don't eat at all, some use drugs, etc. Some beat their wives, some beat their children, some beat their husbands, some bury the pain within themselves, and my husband chose to beat me. I recall the many times he'd hit me. He would have this cold demonic look on his face. It was as if though he became another person.

I thought he was this awful person but now I realized we are all the same we all have issues, we all deal with circumstances our own way. We are all as filthy rags in the eyesight of God. Each time we respond to a situation the wrong way we hurt ourselves or someone else. Although we might never stoop to hitting someone dealing with our problems the wrong way still has consequences. He came in as if nothing had happened. The first thing he did was came and stood over us not knowing if I was alive or dead. Well, I didn't keep him in suspense I soon turned over as if to say, "You didn't kill me."

He awoke the children and fed them and put them in their beds. Soon he came and lay beside me and I fell asleep with quiet, silent tears running down my face.

The next day we were in church first thing Sunday morning. No one would have ever guessed what had gone on the night before.

The day was nearing when God would bring us out of this trailer. If my memory serves me right this was the last time I was hit in the trailer.

CHAPTER 15

A JOURNEY AROUND THE COUNTRY

WE WERE INVITED BACK TO our former home church in Houston, Texas where my son preached a five day revival. The local news channels came and interviewed us and before we knew it we was on all the news channels. My son had also made the local news where we lived when he preached his first sermon.

After returning home my husband wrote Jet magazine and they called us one morning and asked to do the story about our son.

We agreed to their terms and in a matter of weeks they were scheduled to come. We did not want them to come to the trailer. We started praying and although it was a government funded home, God gave us a better home in the nick of time. It's absolutely amazing how God allowed things to fall in place. The same local preacher whom provided us with the car to get to Houston, Texas invited my son to preach revival Sunday at his church in a little town in Hazlehurst, Mississippi. By now we had moved but we did not have anything but our clothes in the house.

There was a preacher there visiting that Sunday. He drove up in a brand new Jaguar, and immediately I thought he was very arrogant. I could not have ever been more wrong. This taught me a lifelong lesson about judging a person because of their worldly possessions.

After church was over he came over and introduced himself. He was one of the most humble men I'd ever met and he remains the same today. He invited my son to come and preach at his church the next Sunday. It was another revival. The word had spread that the eight year old preacher would be preaching in Bogue Chitto, MS., the following Sunday. There was barely standing room in the church. After church we talked to the preacher not knowing who he really was. He was founder of an Outreach Ministry. My husband told him the circumstances of us coming here and how Jet was coming and we had nothing in our house. God used this pastor and his church members to furnish every room in the house. He had a warehouse where he gave away everything a person had need of, food, furniture, money, clothes, even a free medical clinic. His ministry has grown even bigger now; he has helped thousands throughout the United States.

I felt so good. The children felt good. We were in a good home again. I was thrilled to be off the floor and in a bed again. They gave us sheets, towels; they filled the kitchen with food, dishes, silverware, pots and pans. Things were finally looking up for us.

This preacher gave me my first set of real china and he even gave me a mink Stoll.

Well, the night finally came for the Jet magazine people to come. We were all excited. We had so much fun hanging out with them. Not in a million years would I have ever believed we would leave from living in a condemned trailer to appearing in the Jet magazine. God had a plan for us. We appeared on four national television shows after the Jet story came out. We got calls from all over the United States and before I knew it God had made out little Stair steppers mini little stars. They preached and sung in almost every city in Mississippi and in some of the largest cities and largest churches in the United States. The next three or four years was a financial success. We had lived in the best hotels, churches rented luxury cars for us to travel in (we chose not to fly) we were even chauffeured in limousines. God had taken us from two years of poverty to a life of fame and fortune.

We loved the opportunity to go and sing and preach everywhere. I can say from me and my children it came from a pure heart. In spite what we had gone through one thing for sure we loved God with all of our hearts and was pleased to do his will. Although, my children has not traveled as much lately they are still singing, but my sons are still preaching and I believe they have made a lifelong commitment to forever live for God. Even in our messed up, screwed up marriage something good came from it.

Traveling to all these strange places was a joy but there was sometimes some down sides. There was still secrets, still pain, things was still concealed deep within me.

On more than one occasion I was beaten while being out of state doing crusades, on one occasion we had just left a three day crusade in Sioux City, Iowa and was on our way back to Mississippi. We stopped for snacks at a convenient store. He knew each child's favorite snack. However, on this night one of my daughters decided she wanted her older brother's favorite snack (bar-b-que corn chips). Her daddy said, give them to her. Of course my son started crying. Before we knew it my husband pulled off the street to a dark deserted parking lot. He made my son get out and proceeded to drive away. My oldest daughter was screaming "Don't leave him!" Don't leave him! Without thinking I grabbed the steering wheel forcing him to stop the car. He put the car in reverse and went back to get him but not before hitting me several times. At the moment we all thought he would have really left him. Now, when I think about it I guess he was trying to scare him.

While doing a crusade in Rockford, Illinois another incident happened. He wanted the children to sing a song that they had not really learned. They didn't even know all the words. I begged him to choose a song that they knew. We argued about it. He started to hit me and as he grabbed for me he scratched a deep scar in my face. He said he was canceling the crusade and going back to Mississippi. He was planning to leave us in Rockford. He left the hotel leaving me to wonder how I was going to get me and my children back home. My heart pounded all day long but somewhere in my mind I knew he was coming back. I got the children dressed for church and myself, I was hoping and praying he would return. About an hour before church was to start he came back. He had bought several kinds of face powder for me to cover the scar on my face. It worked. No one at the church suspected a thing.

Now, I know if you are scratched, bruised, black eyes, etc. Do not sit at home and hide. Get out let people see what you are going through. Someone somewhere will help you. Even if you are married to one of the most prominent preachers in the world, please do not keep your abuse a secret, make it known. Hiding it will not help you or your spouse. Abusers need help and keeping their secret is only prolonging your pain and theirs. I know you have to be careful how you deal with this situation. Seek God's guidance ask him to help you know what to do and how to do it.

Pastors, preachers, teachers, prophets, evangelists, husbands, and wives if you are abusing your spouse, please stop. Seek help learn to deal with your anger the right way.

Again I ask God to let things be different in this house. I begged him to never let me be beaten in this house but living in this house would prove to be a nightmare. Soon the traveling was over, we weren't getting as many invitations and life was getting back to abnormality. It seems my prayers had not been answered because

I was getting beat pretty frequently. I was back making hair bows to help out financially. Things were going well money wise. At this time we did not have any rent to pay so things were better financially.

Mentally and physically I was plummeting downhill. I was becoming more ill each day it seemed and was hemorrhaging for months at a time. I was extremely anemic and wasn't much good for anything.

In all my years of abuse and hardship life was about to take some drastic challenges. He had taken my sons out of public schools because of all the problems and challenges they faced as young preachers. My oldest son would have anxiety attacks because of being teased and mistreated at school. We tried private schools for several years and eventually he placed both of them in home schooling. This was very hard for me. I was expected to teach them, keep up with homework, sending in their grades, and for a long time even paying for their home schooling. Some days I must admit it was beyond difficult for me. This meant my life again was placed on the back burner, no television, no activities, no talking on the telephone from eight o'clock am to three o'clock pm. It was books, books, and more books, score keys and record keeping. On one occasion I had been bleeding for several months, seemingly I would never stop. We had a section of the living room set up like a classroom and that's where we were to remain. This particular morning my sons got up put on their uniforms, ate breakfast, and started on their books. Well, I was feeling worse than usual so I told them to get their things and come in the family room. I was so sick until I stretched out on the floor; they sat down on the floor beside me. I unknowingly fell asleep. My husband was not working at this time. He woke up I guess an hour or so later and caught me sleeping on the floor. I was lying on my stomach. He walked in and kicked me in my side. As I was trying to get up he kept kicking me, I was so weak until I could not get up so

I tried to push myself into the living room. Just as I got my foot inside the door he slammed the door and please don't ask me how it happened, I can't explain it but he shut my big toe in the door. I started screaming. I could feel the warm blood pouring down my legs, I wasn't concerned about that. I was in serious pain, my toe was closed shut in the door, and I was shaking and shivering. I can't explain to you how bad I was hurting. I started having chills. My sons were just standing there crying. He was telling all of us to be quiet. I was crying out of control, he was yelling telling me to get up. I could not move I was just pointing toward the living room door. I was in shock, I could not say anything. Finally, my son saw it. He couldn't get the door open. He just cried, "Mama Toe is cut off!" My husband open the door, my toe wasn't off but it was cut very deep. Class was over for that day. It seems more and more days of being hit on took place.

Soon, I was just tired. It was getting harder and harder for me to make bows and maintain the household. I was going to the doctor but it seemed I wasn't getting any better.

My husband of course still had needs to be met and although I was sick, I found other ways to make sure his needs was fulfilled. However, my ways would prove not to be enough. Parts of our wedding vows were being tested. The, "for better and for worse," we had done okay with but the in sickness and in health would prove to be another challenge.

One night while out selling hair bows my husband supposedly stopped at this grocery store where he was instantly hired.

We was about to face another challenge that I would have never expected. I must admit to you things that I suspect I have no proof of so it's merely an accusation. He has never come out with a true confession or repentance to me about this matter.

By now my eyes are getting worse I have had my second cornea transplant and (and will later get a third) have been declared disabled and is drawing SSI. My checks were controlled by him and I did not receive anything out of them.

Well life had been a piece of cake until now it seemed. Here's where I hit rock bottom. He started his new job. We now have rent payments plus utilities and car payment.

CHAPTER 16

THE ALLEGED AFFAIR -
THE DEPRESSION

I HAD A DREAM LATE one night of my husband having an affair with this beautiful lady. She was fat but she was beautiful with very light complexioned skin. I told him about the dream telling him to be very prayerful. The dream was so real until I started referring to the lady as big bright. Within a few months our lives took a hundred degree turn for the worse. We were no longer going to church. He was working every Sunday and my children and I had church service every Sunday morning in our family room. The neighbors would tell us how they sat in their homes and looked forward to listening to us on Sunday mornings.

He started coming home later and later and was leaving earlier and earlier. It seemed he never had a day off, he was always gone. I also noticed he would no longer sit at the dinner table with us to eat dinner. Finally I had stopped bleeding and we had what I thought was an active sex life (four to five times weekly). I was in my late thirties and he was in his mid-forties so I thought we were doing alright. I was beginning to feel sadder and sadder and somehow I knew in my spirit something wasn't right. Nothing was the same, we had no communication, and the only thing left between us was sex. Sometimes I truly feel like he practiced on me to get it right for her. The first day I really just got totally depressed he had told me he was going to work from ten to five and would be home by six. Everything in my gut said he was lying so I called his job and his boss said he was off work that day. I got nervous, I wanted to throw up. I was literally sick to my stomach. At about six o'clock p.m. he came home. I was in the bedroom; he walked in looking strange and weird. I asked him where he had been, of course he said work and I immediately knew he was not telling the truth. He sent the children outside to get something out of the van not realizing he had left some evidence behind which was a hotel receipt. He left back out not knowing I now had possession of the receipt. My heart was broken. I had told myself I could take living in poverty sometimes, I could even take being beaten but I could not take him cheating.

I had just gone through one of the toughest times in my life. For four months I literally moved in with my mom to help my other siblings take care of her. She was diagnosed with bone cancer and given six months to a year to live. Our mother was one of the sweetest, kindest, people in the world. We watched her go from a vibrant active woman to bedridden. She suffered greatly. Watching her in such agony had taken a toll on all of us. I was still grieving over my mother for a few weeks when all this took place. How could he do this to me at a time like this? I needed him more than I ever needed anyone. I had lost my precious mama. I wanted him to be there to hold me when I cried. However, instead of holding me in his arms he was holding a stranger. I had days where I would be angry because in all reality he robbed me of my grief. I had no time to deal with my mother's death because I was dealing with what I believed to be a cheating husband. I couldn't grieve for mama because I was grieving for him.

More and more evidence began to surface, hotel keys, phone numbers, room numbers, phone calls, and much more. I would call the hotels when I found the receipts ask if he had checked in the answer was always yes. Sometimes they even described him to me. By now life was awful for me and my five children. We sometimes spent months with no utilities and threats of being evicted. We had a joint account and each month when my check would come in direct deposit, I would have nothing in the account when I called. Finally, I called the bank to see where my money was going. He would use his debit card daily knowing when it would all clear through on the day my check arrived in the bank. This hurt me even more not only was he being unfaithful but I was paying for it. My check paid the hotel fees.

Most days we spent in the house, we were hot, dirty and hungry. Soon I was put in a position to ask neighbors to loan me money to buy food for my children. My children laugh now and say no one could stretch a few dollars like I could. Joking, how I took ten dollars, bought three meals, fed them and three of the neighbors children. Some of the neighbors was aware of our situation and would send pizza, drinks, and ice cream to help out.

Circumstances were pushing me further and further into a state of depression. Most Christians do not like to admit that they become depressed sometimes. I started sleeping more. When I slept I did not have to deal with my problems. There was days when I did not get out of bed. I could not find the courage or the strength to get up. I would lay there in bed and if I wasn't sleeping I was crying. I just could not understand what was happening to me. Soon my coal black hair was turning gray, my peachy skin was once again dark and discolored, I had black circles around my eyes, I had no incentive to comb my hair, some days I did not take a bath or dress myself. For two years I did not look in a mirror. I could not stand to see what I was turning into. There was times when I did not eat or drink anything for days at a time. It got so bad until I would not leave the house. I would send my oldest daughter with a list to the store with the lady across the street. I was losing it and I knew it. I would call my husband at work and beg him to come home after work.

He started to take things from our house, televisions, cameras, anything he could pawn for money. He even took my oldest daughter most prize possession, her keyboard. These items we never saw again.

Sometimes, two of the children would stay up all night waiting to see if he was going to bring food home or not. Sometimes he did, sometimes he didn't. He was beginning to look awful himself. Riotous living was taking a toll on him. He was losing weight, he looked old and tired. He would come home late but he never spent a night away from home.

He had bought some cattle that my daddy was keeping on his land. He sold them one by one. We were losing everything. Having an affair was taking a toll on us every way it could.

I specifically recall something that happened one night. Well actually it was around four o'clock a.m. He decided to be intimate with me. I hated him touching me, I was afraid I might get a disease, but I allowed it because I was still his wife. I was just broken; my heart was in a million pieces, I wanted more than anything in this world to be loved by him. I wanted him to be attracted to me; I wanted him to want me and no one else. I wanted to know how it felt to make love to a person that really loved you. I knew my husband did not love me; he was not attracted to me and did not want me.

I wanted him to want me so bad that he would lie to be with me, he would go to a hotel to be with me, he would miss work to be with me, he would pawn his daughter's keyboard to be with me, I wanted him to want me as much as he wanted HER!

I asked him to pretend that I was her, pretend that he loved me. I could honestly feel the difference, he had never made the type of love he did that morning. I could see passion in his eyes, I felt his heart pounding against mine, we had always had sex but this time we made love.

I was being ignorant but at the moment something was being fulfilled in me. It was not about the sex it was about a few moments of pretending he loved me as much as I loved him. He began speaking out to me, she likes this, she like's when I do such and such. The game had gone too far. I was hearing what I did not want to hear. He really did have someone else and he cared a lot for her, I could feel it in his embracing, I could feel it in the passionate kissing, I could see it in his eyes but more than anything I heard it coming from his mouth. I began to sob uncontrollably. He fell asleep as I lay there hurting worse than ever.

A few hours later he was up and gone saying he had to be to work at ten. I got up, lit the grill and started grilling some chicken. He loved bar-b-que and I thought I would make him happy if I cooked something he liked.

Well, at about eleven thirty a.m. the phone rang and when I answered the person hung up. I looked at the caller-id and it was someone calling from the same hotel he had been going to. I dialed the number back but no one answered. I called his job and his boss told me he called earlier and took the day off. He asked me how I was doing because word was spread on the job that I had cancer. He apologized for the things I was going through. I had suspected he was involved with one of the employees on the job but I had no proof. His boss told me this lady had called in a few minutes after he did and took the day off as well. He went on to say that every time he took off she did too, they took every lunch break together, and if she came in late he came in late. I thanked him for telling me. I tried calling the hotel over and over again but neither of them would answer the phone. I could not finish cooking. That day my two sons learned to bar-b-que.

Until now I had not discussed my situation with anyone. This had been going on for maybe a year now and I'd kept it to myself.

I was in too deep. I was only a minute away from having a breakdown. I knew I needed help. I called my sisters and told them. I begged them to take me to the hotel; I wanted so much to see this lady. They did not take me. Later that night a friend of mine from Houston, Texas called me. We had not been in touch for years but God told her to call. She's very spiritual, a prayer warrior and one who won't let you give up.

I had gone through months of catching him on the phone, months of her calling hanging up. On a few occasions I had even talked to her and she denied the affair. I asked her forgiveness because I could not prove she was the one. My friend from Houston called me every day. By now I'm still progressing downward. I'm sick both mentally and physically. I wanted her to give up on me but she would not. Everyone needs a praying friend like her. She was tough on me, she was hard on me, she was downright mean, but it was all to bring Shirley back to Shirley. I no longer existed in this two year period. I had become this pitiful, desperate broken spirited something. I was spending more time sleeping. Some days my girls would come and lay in the bed with me and we would all just lay there and cry ourselves to sleep.

"Pick yourself up, girl! Get out of that bed, stand on your feet, wake yourself up quit feeling sorry for yourself, and quit feeling sorry for him! God is going to fix it, I refuse to see you breakdown I will not let you go insane! You don't have to pray, I am going to pray for you! Don't try to read your bible; I'm going to read it to you.

I heard this every day from my friend. She prophesied to me things that had come to pass. She even said God showed her he had a king for me someone who was going to treat me like a queen. On Sunday mornings my children would drag me out of bed for our church services. My sisters stopped by on occasions to check on me. My former pastor came and prayed for me. He encouraged me not to give up. He took out hours and ministered to my broken heart. I always say by the grace of God this pastor and my friend saved my life.

For most of these two years I could not and did not pray, some days. I did not read my bible, I had not lost my trust in God, and I just didn't have a mind to do anything.

Have you ever been at a point where you could not pray? I'm so glad that my children and others were praying for me. I know now that when I was moaning and crying the Holy Spirit was praying for me. God saw me, he heard me, and he answered me. Things weren't getting any better but I was learning to cope better.

The bleeding started once again but this time it was worse than ever. My husband got up one morning told me to get dressed because he needed me to go somewhere with him. I would have never guessed we were going to see an attorney. The lawyer did not show up for the appointment so he took me to several others until he found one who agreed to divorce us. He told him to come back the next week with half the money and he would start the procedures. I stood there crying and begging the lawyer and him to please don't do this to me. I told the lawyer how much I loved him and wanted my marriage to work. I said I wasn't signing divorce papers, never. I felt myself becoming very weak and faint. I could feel the blood rushing down in clots. I knew I was much sicker than I had ever been. I rushed out to the car and got in. He soon came out. By this time blood was everywhere. I told him to take me to the emergency room. He drove up, let me out, and left to get the children from school. I was extremely embarrassed. My clothes were soiled, I was miserable. Soon I was checked in and my gynecologist was on his way.

He wasn't pleased that I was there alone so he tried several times to get in touch with him. He took me straight to surgery to stop the bleeding. My husband showed up only when I was discharged. It was a year later when I was doing better both mentally and physically my doctor told me that day I had miscarried a baby. I was forty years old and just thought no way. He showed me in my records. As a result of the affair an innocent baby died. God knew I could not handle having a baby at such a stressful time in my life.

These were two difficult years for me. I thought I was above depression. I thought I was so holy and so righteous until I couldn't be depressed. After all I'd lived through abuse, through poverty nothing could get me down.

I was wrong, something had happened to me that I couldn't fix. I was broken. Secrets that I'd kept hidden all this time was coming out. Even then I thought God was going to punish me. You are disgracing a preacher. You telling things that you should not. I was living in denial. It was time for me to live again. I had to find myself. Even then I was only telling some of the story. No one still knew how bad things really were for me. I still had secrets but at least the ice had been broken.

Eventually, he transferred jobs and seemingly whatever he was doing stopped. We did a few revivals after this and somewhere within the year we joined another church. The church was small and it took some time but eventually the church grew on us. We began to like being members there.

During the two year period there were not many occasions that I was hit on. Now, those things ended the abuse started again. My children are getting old enough now to really be angry at what's going on. On one occasion they told a family member.

Now, another form of abuse has started. It's a frame of mind. I have lost all trust and most respect for him. Every time he touches me I wonder is he thinking of her. I say I have forgiven him but I still can't get over what he had done. It's a new hurt and pain now. All had been lost in our marriage. Sometimes I brought up what he had done. I always suspected the worse in him. I didn't really believe anything he said. I could not bring myself to initiate sex with him. Sometimes, I didn't respond to sex with him. I felt cold and sterile toward him. I use to hold him, touch on him and now I just want to crawl to my side of the bed and be left alone. Kissing him made me nauseated. It's getting harder and harder for me to say I love you to him. I use to cherish our conversations together, now, I avoided them. There were times I loved him being home, now I'm glad when he leaves. I cooked all his favorite meals but now it doesn't matter if he eats or not. When he hits me it's a loss of control. This situation was well thought out, it was planned and plotted and now that you decides to call it off you just want me to welcome you back with open arms. Well, I found I couldn't do it. I thought I wanted him back so much but when I got him back I discovered nothing was the same. The man that I once married and loved no longer existed. I'd forgiven the physical abuse but this time he had overstepped his boundaries. I can tell he's disappointed. He's use to getting his way with me. He's shocked and can't get over the fact that this time it's hard for me to forgive and move on. I'm trying but he must try too.

All these mixed emotions have left me feeling like a hypocrite. Why can't I love him? Why can't I just move on from this? How can I say the love of God is in me and I want forget what has happened?

The depression had ended and all sorts of things are setting in on me. When we pass the hotel where most of the things took place my heart breaks all over again. I cry every time. On occasions I timed the minutes he was from home. Only twelve to fifteen minutes on the interstate. Why couldn't he just come home to me, instead of meeting her there? I questioned everything about my womanhood. I began to think it happened because I was fat, because I was a virgin when we married, I probably didn't know enough to please him. I wondered what would they do when they arrived at the hotel, who arrived first, did the first one who arrived get undressed and wait in bed for the other one, did he pick her up in our vehicle, I wondered did they kiss, what positions did they make love in, did she do things I could not or would not do.

I thought these things would never leave me. I thought for the rest of my life I would be hurting. It was like losing my mother, it never has stopped hurting me but I've learned to deal with it. I think I'll forever feel some pain from this but I am over the hurt of it all.

We have fallen into a financial hardship because of all of this and are now faced with being evicted from our home. The stress of trying to get over the affair and our financial situation is getting the best of me. Once again we are forced back on welfare (food stamps). My husband did not want to get stamps but yet he wasn't making enough to supply all our needs. Against his will and for the sake of the children I made an appointment to apply for assistance. On the morning of the appointment it was raining cats and dogs. He refused to take me to the appointment. Although, I had not ever road on the Jatran that morning I was determined to make things better for my children. My oldest son and I walked to the bus stop through knee deep water. When we made it to the appointment we were soaked from our head to our feet. It didn't matter, we were there and we received the help I was seeking and at least for the next year we never had to worry about food.

CHAPTER 17

LIVING LIFE ON THE EDGE

WE ONLY HAD A FEW weeks to move to another place and we were having a difficult time finding somewhere to live. Eventually, God blessed us with a bigger and better home than we had ever lived in and within two years we were completely welfare free.

A few weeks before moving to our new home I had major surgery where I had to receive four units of blood. It took several months for me to recover. I had come very close to dying from losing most of the blood in my body. There had been a few instances where he hit me after the surgery but this particular time stood out. He was working the night shift on his job so he did not get to attend church regularly. Often people would ask about him and when we would get home I would tell him. Well, one Sunday this man asked about him and asked what shift he worked. Without giving any thought about it, I answered him. Well, of course when I made it home I told him who asked about him and what they asked. He freaked out, he went in a rage. I did not understand what made him so angry. He overflowed with wrath. Although, he knew I was recovering from surgery and was on medication to restore my blood, he started beating me out of control. I was very anemic so I was too weak to do anything. For the first time in our twenty one years of being married at that time, I decided to fight him back. I don't ever recall a time when I had the courage to fight him back. Today was different. I was just tired of being beat. Of course he was getting the best of me. He had me on the floor beating me to death. He hit me with a chair and anything he could get his hands on but I was still trying to kick and hit him. My oldest son ran in to try to stop him, he made him go outside threatening if he didn't he would kill him. I was having problems breathing, I could feel myself about to faint but I was begging my son to get out. He grabbed the phone and went outside. I think he had made up his mind to call the police but something took place before he could. Somehow, I got enough strength to get on my feet; I made it almost to the hallway before he could grab me. He kept saying I'm going to kill you today. He told me I should not have discussed his job with anyone. He found a big thick board from somewhere and was about to put my lights out. When I saw the board I knew if I didn't get up my life would probably be over that day. As I tried to pull myself from the floor, I heard my third daughter saying, "This don't make no damn sense," she was angry she was downright mad and she had had enough. My baby girl was crying and screaming like she had done since she was a little girl when she saw him hitting me. The younger two would scream and cry and run and hide wherever they could. The older three would remain as close as possible wherever I was.

Well, that day she came over and said, "Don't hit my mama anymore! Don't hit her, I mean it! She started wrestling him for the board as he drew back to hit me, something happen! My youngest daughter stopped crying her and my oldest daughter grabbed the board also just a split second before it reached my head. They wrestled him until the board fell. Just as the board fell I passed out. When I came to myself my five "angels" had me stretched out on the sofa taking care of me. We all had had enough that day. I knew it was all over the violence was finally over. Being slapped around would never happen again. Something happened that day that was a new beginning.

CHAPTER 18

BECOMING A NEW ME!

REVEALING EVERY SECRET!

The next day came and I stepped all the way out of my secret world. I talked to two ministers; I told them what had happened. From that day I was no longer ashamed to talk about my life. I knew it was time to help other ladies and other people but I didn't know how.

For twenty-one years I had prayed and asked God why he was allowing me to go through such a rough marriage. Why did three months after being married he allowed my preacher husband to beat me. I prayed daily, constantly and I never received an answer and nothing ever changed.

Two years ago in the middle of the night, God spoke to me in a vision, "This is why, I allowed you to go through the abuse, I want you to write a book about the abuse and it is going to help people all over the world." He gave me the title, "The Secret Life of a Preacher's Wife."

For months I prayed and I sought God for direction. I wanted to make sure I had heard the voice of God. I started working on this book over a year ago. Chapters have been found and destroyed by him. He did not want me to write this book. He's ashamed of all the awful things he did to me. He asked me to make a decision between him and writing this book. Really, what he was saying is choose between me and God. It took me some time, I've put off writing. I've begged him to change his mind. He refuses. It will be a struggle for me maybe. I have no income and right now nowhere to go, but I trust God. He told me to write this book and I must obey him.

I want you my readers to know, I'm not professing to be perfect I have many faults. I love my husband, I will always love him, but I've learned in the last year I'm no longer in love with him. I am not leaving him with the intentions of being with someone else.

I have forgiven him for everything wrong over these twenty-five years that has happened between the two of us. I would love to remain his friend but he said that will be impossible.

I hope he finds someone very soon that will fill the emptiness and void in him that I could not for twenty-five years.

This book has not been written with the intent of hurting, embarrassing, tearing down, or humiliating him.

God told me to reveal our secrets to help the world. Someone, once said to me, "For every day that book is not published, one lady is still abused; one lady goes to prison for defending herself, one lady dies at the hand of her abuser.

This paragraph is devoted strictly to preacher's wives. I know that I'm not the only one that has lived in this situation. There are many of you, some of you have mega husbands in mega churches, some of you have radio ministries, television ministries, some of you might be in small churches, or married to associate ministers. It's time for you "Preachers Wives!" to reveal your secret lives. Come out of the closet. Let it be known. He needs help, you need help. I know this book will probably destroy some marriages, but I truly believe for everyone destroyed there will be ten healed. I know what it's like to come in church on Sunday mornings in the fancy hats and fancy clothes, smiling and acting, (act - ing) as if you are in the happiest marriage in the world. I've done that too. I know that I am not the only preacher's wife whose husband has had an affair, whose husband is neglectful when it comes to supporting his family and I'm not the only one who has missed church because of scratches and bruises. Preachers, you need to admit you have problems you have faults like everyone else. Admit you give all the counseling but sometimes you need counseling too. Ladies, preacher's wives we live with the guilt of thinking if we say anything we will tear our husbands down, or we think we love them so much we want say anything. Sometimes the abuse has caused us to have such low self-esteem until we think we can't get anyone else. Sometimes it's all the above and so much more.

Well, over the last few chapters I have talked a lot about my deep dark secrets. I hope when this book is complete it will have completely changed the lives of preachers, preachers wives, women, men, boys and girls all over the world.

I will lose a man to gain the freedom of many of you. In reality my marriage was over the first day I was beaten about the chocolate pie. God can restore my marriage, he can heal it, and he can give me more than I ever had in this marriage but it takes two willing people. Men and women abusers I know some of you are going to get help. I believe you are tired of being mean and hateful, tired of keeping secrets and this book is going to give you the opportunity to seek help.

There is much danger in staying in abusive situations. It affects every person that's involved. I know someday there will be some negative affects even in the life of our five children. It is always my prayer that they will keep God in their lives and that he will keep them from hurt, harm, and danger and that they will not bring hurt, harm or danger to themselves or anyone else.

My oldest daughter was involved once with a young man that was all wrong for her. He was violent and very quick tempered. Statistics has shown that girls who grow up in violent homes are more likely to marry someone the same way. I'm thankful she saw the signs and moved on. She remained a virgin until she married a wonderful man a year ago.

Another danger in staying in an abusive situation is miscalculating the intention of other men or women who are kind and nice to you. A year ago something happened to me. Something that I thought would not possibly happen to me. My husband was my very first boyfriend, my first kiss, my first everything. I had never been interested in anyone else. However, as I said a year ago things changed. The secret I'm about to reveal now might change some people view of me, it will cause some of you to wonder, some of you will judge me, some of you will be like my husband and accuse me of having an affair, and I have not had an affair and have no intentions of doing so.

Another secret revealed. The years of mental abuse took its toll. The years of being called out of my name being made to feel ugly and unattractive made me vulnerable, I guess to nice compliments.

I met a man who was one of the kindest men I've ever known. Some might not find him attractive but he's very attractive to me inside and out. We talked a lot or he more talked and I listened, I enjoyed his conversations and if I could I'd hear him talk all day and night. My self-esteem was at zero on the charts when I met him. Where my husband called me old and gray headed, he would tell me he liked my hair. He would tell me I was radiant and my husband never said anything at all. I noticed within this, I was beginning to have some wrong feelings for this man. When I see him I get butterflies, I think about him a lot, (more than I should), and I dream about him, I realize now that something was happening. I have fallen deeply in love with him. I'm sure he does not feel the same way so even if it could nothing will come of my feelings. The years of being neglected has caused something to happen that I feel very ashamed about, I cry a lot about it, when I think of him I feel bad for having such thoughts. I have sought counseling and advice for this matter and although I've been told this is pretty much a normal situation. I still live with guilt.

Ladies, I want you to know this can happen to any of us. Years of neglect can lead to things not pleasing to God. I constantly beat myself up for allowing myself to be in this situation. Sometimes, I wish I'd never engaged in the first conversation with this person. It started innocently on my part. I'm a person whom loves talking to most people. I try being a friendly person. I thought I could talk with him just like I had with hundreds of people before. We talked a lot about our children, we sometimes talked about our spouses, but more than anything we talked about the bible and both our love for God.

The thing that I despised the most in my life is now happening to me. I despised people that cheated or got involved with another person's relationship even if you just called yourselves friends.

Well, I considered him a friend but after a year things changed. And although we've never done more than shook hands I feel guilty as if I had an affair.

A friend told me what I feel for this person is not love but infatuation. I find it difficult for a person to tell someone else what they are feeling. I have loved my husband for twenty-four and a half years and some part of me will forever love him. However, I have lost that love that binds us together as one, it's no longer there and my feeling for the other person did not cause this, it came from all the years of mental and physical abuse.

It is absolutely amazing to me what words can do to a person. For instance, I've heard my whole life words can make you or break you. I find this to be true. When I started engaging in conversations with this person my spirit had been broken by negative words coming from my husband. If you hear something long enough you start to believe it. I am not the most beautiful person you'll ever meet; I definitely do not have an hour glass figure. I am an overweight black woman whom is often reminded daily of my short comings. Words had caused me to believe in spite of how I combed my hair or how I dressed, I was still fat and ugly. These words had turned me into a crippled, broken, down hearted person who kept my head down. The thing that I enjoy most in life is smiling. Years of poverty and neglect has even caused damage to my teeth which forces me to smile less. Even my smile had been taken away. Negative words had strong impact on me.

However, when I met this person he told me my smile made his day. All the negative words turned into positive ones when they came from him and before I knew it my self-esteem was returning. I say often the one good thing that has come from this person I truly believe God himself used him to help me get back my self-esteem. I'm an overweight black woman, I am not the most beautiful person you'll ever meet, I do not have an hour glass figure but I am human and I'm God's child and now I feel good about myself. I look in the mirror now, I love to get dressed now and I feel so much better about myself. Although, I believe I'm in love with this person the most important thing is he helped showed me how to love myself. I thought certain things could not happen to me. I was self-righteous, holier than Thou and very judgmental to other people who committed certain sins. Now I know I'm not any better than anyone else, I too am subject to make mistakes.

Through counseling I found out it will take time to get over this situation. I was told how to pray and what to pray for and in time whatever God' will is for my life it will take place.

Be careful of the friends you choose when you are in a vulnerable situation. Feeling unwanted and unloved by your spouse can lead to things you need to avoid. Things such as lust, adultery, unclean thoughts, wishful thinking, dreams and all sorts of things God might not be pleased with.

I found myself in this situation of being in love with an unavailable married man. I talk to God about this often, I beg for his mercy and forgiveness. I discussed this matter with my husband. I was honest with him. I asked him to pray with me and for me that God's grace would help me to overcome this situation. He asked many questions of me all of which I answered with truth and honesty. I think the most profound question he asked was, if I could, would I sleep with this person. I told him no, and my answer was both true and honest. By the grace of God I would not. However, I believe many neglected spouses have affairs because of mental issues they have dealt with.

I can't stretch enough to those that abuse others the anguish, the pain, the heartache, the bitterness, the scars, inside and out, the doubt, the fear, the nervousness, the disgust, the dirtiness, the darkness, the emptiness and so much more that you bring on your victims.

Pastors, preachers, men, please realize what you are doing to your wife. God say we are the weaker vessels and we are. I don't care if we are perfect, underweight or overweight we are naturally weaker than a man. When you beat us there's emptiness inside that nothing or no one fills. It's a feeling of self-worthiness. It's something that talk shows neither secular nor spiritual can fill. Although, the positive words can change your attitude sometimes the emptiness will creep back upon you. You will be around people and you'll hear them laughing and having fun and sometimes in the back of your mind you feel the emptiness. You feel superficial. Sometimes in church and other places, I look around at different ladies and I can spot out the ones that are being mistreated. I can even see it in a man that's mistreated and unhappy. You know even the world knows the danger in married people mistreating one another. If you ever watch a movie or even soap operas and you see a married couple get in an argument or one start staying at the office more than they should, then they bring another lady or man in the scene most of us know what the plot is going to be. The spouse that's feeling neglected most likely has an affair with that person. Well, that's television but in all reality it's happening in marriages every day. We are cheating every day and sometimes it's simply just from having uncontrollable lust.

A lack of communication among spouses creates many problems. I know there are times when my husband and I were angry at one another it might be days, weeks or even months before he'd say a word to me. I am a person whom for the most part cannot stay mad at anyone. So, a few hours would pass by I'd be in his face apologizing or asking forgiveness even if I was not the one at fault. I just wanted to make up and not be angry.

I recall something that happen a little over a year ago. During this time one of the most tragic events had taken place in my life. My oldest brother, was in the hospital and we were expecting him to die. He was very, very ill. On a late Saturday night we got news that my baby brother, whom was two years older than me had been in a very serious accident. He supposedly had an aneurysm to the brain and had broken most every bone in his body. He stayed in a coma for about thirty days before going home to be with God. Our oldest brother lived and thank God is doing fine.

Needless to say, this shook us as a family. On the night my brother left us I came home heartbroken. My husband had had a close relationship with him over the years. As I walked through the door he stood there needing me as much as I needed him. (My two sisters and two brothers and I spent every day and night between hospitals with our brothers.) We literally fell into one another arms crying uncontrollably. That night we slept in one another arms and for the rest of the week we did the same. For the first time we were being to one another what we needed to be. We buried my brother on that Saturday and for the next two days everything was perfect.

However, something happened that changed everything. His cell phone rang around 1:00 p.m. The Spirit was urging me to get up and stand by my bedroom door. I sat there on the sofa talking to my children as the spirit continued, go stand by your door. I was making some pillows on my sewing machine, so I pushed it aside and walked down the hallway toward my bedroom door. He had closed the door but I was still able to hear him talking and what I heard was not good news. He was saying baby this and baby that. I was thinking to myself, he's talking to a woman. I was in denial that it could possibly be another affair. He had been so down on me for the thing I had confessed to him. I went and stood in my daughter's bedroom next to mine where I could hear even better because he was sitting next to the wall between our bedrooms. I heard something that shocked me so much until I had to sit on the bed to keep from falling, "Baby, you know how much I love you, and I told you I'm just here with that Negro until the money I'm expecting come through. The WEDDING is still on and I'm definitely going to marry you. I love you and want to be married to you. That Negro is trying to change her mind about signing the divorce papers but don't worry she is going to sign them. I told you as soon as this money come through from the place I'm expecting it we are getting married. Baby you know I love you and want to be with you. The lawyers' office is closed today, but first thing Monday morning I'm filing for the divorce."

Well, for months he had been begging me to sign the divorce papers, but I had refused. I was still thinking in spite of everything God wanted our marriage to work. Well, I walked in the room I could not stand to hear anymore. I grabbed his cell phone out his hands and pushed him into the wall. She heard the commotion and hung the phone up. I don't know who she was, I have never found out who she was. I always ask God to let me know but so far he has not shown me. He could not deny anything because he knew I had heard everything. After all the months of him degrading me about feelings that I had not acted on he had been involved with this person. I could tell from all the things he said she was getting tired and was ready to be married to him. They discussed how happy they were going to be and how happy they were when they saw one another.

Well, our marriage had been everything but happy and although we sometimes had joyous occasions together I don't remember many days in twenty five years where we were happy together all day and night.

Well, here it was one week after burying my brother, a few years after burying my mom and dad, and after the death of our baby girl or boy here I was again unable to grieve for my brother because I had to once again deal with these issues. That night he moved to the bottom of the bed where he slept for the next six months. First thing Monday morning he was on the phone with his attorney just as he had promised her, I don't know if he's still involved with her or not all I know is he became silent toward me and as hard as this might be for you to believe he did not say one word to me for six months.

If he wanted sex he came to the top of the bed had sex, didn't say a word, go back to the bottom and fell asleep. Christmas, our wedding anniversary, and Mother's Day passed by and he still didn't say a word. On Sunday if he was able to attend church he did not even look at me.

This sounds both sad and hypocritical but I know there are other preachers and their wives doing the same thing. Some of you are sleeping in separate rooms, living separate lives and maybe on

Sunday morning you come together like a happy couple and go to church and pretend.

I'm glad my husband no longer pretends. It used to be when we went to church together, he would introduce me as his friend, his companionship, his sweetheart, his wife, Shirley better known as The Mother Goose of them all. I was called the Mother Goose because of having five stair step children. However, now if I go to church with him he does not even recognize me. Recently, I attended a revival service he was conducting, I attended four nights, every night the preachers introduced their wives but not once did he mention I was there. I guess the pastor of the church was offended by this so he asked me to stand and be recognized.

I was not offended by my husband actions. He does not consider me his wife anymore, he tells people we are divorced or in the process of divorcing. Under the eyes of the law we are still married. In our hearts we are not.

If there is any hope of healing for our marriage we need to savage it now. He blames this man for the failure of our marriage but he knows that this marriage was in trouble years ago.

Some preachers I believe have too much pride to admit they have faults, For instance most of you that hit your wife; you try to twist it and make it be our fault. It's never a woman's fault that you hit her no matter what she does. It's all about controlling your own temper. Some of you have the nerves to use the scripture to justify your abuse. Your favorite small quote, "A woman supposed to obey her husband and if she don't!"

CHAPTER 19

THE CONCLUSION

MEN HAVE MISINTERPRETED GOD'S WORD for years, sometimes for their own gain and benefit.

Too long have we misused God's word to stay in situations we should have been left. We need to learn what God say about certain situations.

We too need to learn from God's word that not everyone that's married was joined together by God.

For answers to the following questions please consult your pastor. You can consider utilizing these questions for group discussions in your women ministries as well.

Is there ever a time divorce is permissible?

Is there a time when our prayers and our wants keep us in a situation God is trying to free us from?

Does a man have the right to hit his wife according to the scripture?

What to do when the love is gone in your marriage?

Can Christians remarry and be in God's will?

Will a real man of God hit his wife?

Will a true preacher, mentally, physically or spiritually hurt his wife?

What should a preacher do if he's married to the wrong person?

When to know when enough is enough?

What affect does an abusive marriage have on children?

What should you do if because of the years of abuse you fall in love with someone else?

Can God restore a marriage that has so many downfalls?

Does God expect all Christian's marriages to last?

How to seek spiritual guidance when you are being abused?

How to get your self-esteem back after years of put down?

Should you tell your spouse if you had an affair?

Should you tell your spouse if you have feelings for another person?

How to know if your spouse really loves you?

Should married couples who have children remain sociable after divorce?

If your spouse has sex with someone outside the marriage do you still have to have sex with them?

How can a person truly forgive their spouse for having an affair?

How should Christians deal with depression?

How to heal the scars inwardly of years of both mental and physical abuse?

What to do when your spouse denies his or her actions?

These have been questions that have plagued me for years. I've told you my story; I've told you my secrets. This book is not intended to talk about the happy or joyous times. There were some days when I had some hours of happiness. My husband has a good side to him. He has instilled a lot of good values in his five children. They would not be as successful as they are if it wasn't for their Father. I've had years of loving him with all my heart. I've cherished him, trusted him, and obeyed him. I've put twenty five years in hoping for a good marriage. I've loved him in spite of the good and the bad. He has helped bought most of the material things I possess. He has bought me the best lotions and colognes. We've had hardships but there are times we have flourished in money as well. As far as I'm concerned we've sometimes had a good sex life. Although, we have never talked about the abuse because he doesn't admit to it, we have had good communication skills at times. I feel we somehow connected spiritually in our marriage for many years but we never had a physical or mental connection. I'm a firm believer that it takes all three to make a strong marriage. There was a time when we had a good prayer life together. I think I have been such a protector of him that I too only brought more pain to him. I believe if I had told someone sooner what was going on we could have saved our marriage. I refuse to say anything negative about his upbringing because I did not grow up in his home but I believe something happened in his childhood that shaped him into the person he is. I can admit about my childhood at the expense of possibly making my siblings angry. I believe I became protector and so forgiving and so vulnerable because I watched my mom who was never hit on by our father, and they never argued a lot but yet he involved himself in something that was mental abuse to my mother. I watched her take things with a loving forgiving spirit. If this rubbed off on me and caused me to probably take more than I should then somewhere people, who are abusive grew up around something they should not have. There are men who grew up with mothers who was demanding and controlling and at young ages they decide they are not going to take anything off a woman. This usually results in him beating his wife to control her.

My husband often tells me and even before marrying him that he likes a lot of attention. I tried everything within myself to please him, I literally kissed his butt to please him but I now realize something was missing in his life from someone else and it's nothing me or any other lady can do to replace it. I too had something missing from someone in my life. For years I had prayed that God would allow me to know what it felt like to be the special child to my mom. Mama loved me with all her heart but I had never felt special. God granted me my wish the four months my mom was on her death bed, I was special to her, we had closeness and a connection we had never had. I would sing to her and read to her and she'd look at me with her big brown eyes and for the first time I knew how much she really loved me. That's what's missing in my husbands' life. Somewhere he has given out much love and hasn't received it back. I know now he might not admit it, but he's vulnerable, he's sad, he's scared, he didn't get all the love he needed as a child. Preachers most of you that are beating your wives please admit, it's not about your wives, it's about you. As I write it's like a mystery being solved to me. I recall so many times when I would be right about a situation and he would be wrong that's the time he would beat me the most. If I appeared smarter about something than him he would beat me. It's all about the confusion, the low self-esteem you have. Preachers you feel low, you feel stupid, and you feel insecure so you try to bring your wives down to your level. I have not written this book with intentions of hurting my husband or any other preacher or man. I would never by the grace of God keeping me intentionally do anything to hurt anyone. To my family and his family, to all our friends, church members and his students, this book is not about finding an excuse to hate him or me. It's really about loving, and forgiving. More than anything it's about getting out of a situation that's causing you lots of hurt and pain. We can search the world and never will we find a perfect marriage but we will find happy ones. If you are being mentally or physically abused and you are tired of it, get out, trust God. If your marriage is meant to be, with time you'll get back together. It is unfair to your spouse, to your children, but most of all it's unfair to you to stay in a situation where you are always unhappy, sad, and downright miserable. I saw my husband sometimes when I walked in the room his whole expressions changed the sight of me ruined his day and sometimes he did me the same way. My prayers are with him and the next person he chooses to be with. I hope he admits the issues and deals with them so that his next spouse will find the joy and happiness with him she deserves. I look forward to a new life with my children, hopefully someday my grandchildren and a closer committed walk with God. I look forward to an outreach ministry that will focus on preacher wives who are willing to admit their abuse, all ladies, teenagers; I look forward to doing lectures on avoiding abuse, etc. I pray God open doors for me to go in and share my story to churches and organizations all over America. Also I'm hoping to work on my own personal self, physically, mentally and spiritually. I hope reading my story, "The Secret Life of a Preachers Wife," has somehow impacted you and opened your mind to a change. If I can reach one abuser and influence you to quit inflicting your pain on others I will have accomplished a part of my goal. If this book will keep one lady out of prison, will help keep one lady out of their grave then I will have accomplished another part of my goal. If one preacher will stand before his congregation and say I have been beating my wife but I want to change, I will have accomplished another part of my goal. If this book causes one young lady to look for the warning signs in her boyfriend and causes her to go her separate way then I will have accomplished a part of my goal.

If this book will cause my children to come to me and say mom I'm glad you revealed your secrets and I still love you, I will have accomplished a part of my goal. If this book will cause my sisters and brothers to go to my husband and say I forgive you for all you have done, I will have accomplished a part of my goal. If my in-laws read this book and not hate me I will have accomplished a part of my goal. If every Christian who reads this book forgives me and my husband for our short comings I will have accomplished a part of my goal. If this book will cause some sinner to cry out to God to be saved from their sins I will have accomplished a part of my goal.

If this book will cause my husband, whom I'm no longer living with to admit to his downfalls, his mental, physical and spiritual abuse towards me, if he reads this book and makes no attempt to hurt me in any way, if he allows this book to help him heal then I, Shirley will have accomplished all my goals.

"God Bless All of You"

My Readers

Contact: Ms. Shirley

For

Seminars, Lectures or Speaking Engagements

E-Mail

shirleysecretsrevealed@aol.com

If you are being abused please contact the police department, the domestic organization in your city; your police department should have their number. Please e-mail me from anywhere in the world, and I'll do everything I can to help you get out safely.